Bite ... 3

Edited by Cecil Gray

Nelson
Caribbean

Thomas Nelson and Sons Ltd
Nelson House Mayfield Road
Walton-on-Thames Surrey
KT12 5PL UK

51 York Place
Edinburgh
EH1 3JD UK

Nelson Blackie
Wester Cleddens Road
Bishopbriggs
Glasgow
G64 2NZ UK

Thomas Nelson (Hong Kong) Ltd
Toppan Building 10/F
22A Westlands Road
Quarry Bay Hong Kong

Thomas Nelson Australia
102 Dodds Street
South Melbourne
Victoria 3205 Australia

Nelson Canada
1120 Birchmount Road
Scarborough Ontario
M1K 5G4 Canada

ISBN 0-17-566388-2
NPN 9 8 7 6 5 4 3 2 1

Printed in Hong Kong.
Typeset by Litho Link Limited, Welshpool, Powys.

ii

To the poets of the West Indies
– past, present and future.

How to Eat a Poem
Eve Merriam

Don't be polite.
Bite in.
Pick it with your fingers and lick the juice that may run
    down your chin.
It is ready and ripe now, whenever you are.

You do not need a knife or fork or spoon
or plate or napkin or tablecloth.

For there is no core
or stem
or rind
or pit
or seed
or skin
to throw away.

Contents

1 Growing Up

2 Conflicts and Crises

3 Struggle and Survival

4 The Passing of Time

5 Creativity and Endeavour

LEVEL TWO

1 Love and Friendship

2 The Faces of Struggle

3 Beliefs and Values

4 Home and Abroad

5 Choices and Freedom

6 Creativity and Endeavour

7 Dilemmas

To Young Readers of Poems

The poems in *Bite In* have been selected to introduce you to the pleasures that people get from language. Each one was chosen to give you pleasure from just reading it, although some questions for class disscussion and private thinking are suggested. Many poems need very little discussion. But to take a poem in as part of your experience you have to read it over several times aloud, and you might have to put some thought into it.

Do not use the discussion questions, however, as a kind of test. They are to help you to be more aware of things you might miss and to increase the pleasure you can get from the poem.

Like other art forms, poetry expresses in a memorable way what it means to live in the world. You enjoy it better when you can see how skilfully words are used to get you to sense an experience and the feeling the poem attaches to it. For instance, how the words are chosen to make you hear a *rhythm*. That is sometimes called the *metre* of the poem.

As a class you can get much enjoyment doing a choral orchestration of a suitable poem, by arranging certain lines to be said by different groups, by individuals, and by the whole class, just as a song is arranged by a choir.

In talking about a poem you should look for the things that poets do with words, such as how they make comparisons – sometimes called something by some other name – to make a reader attend to a particular feature or quality in the thing. For example, in his poem *To Build our House* (*Bite In 1*), A.L. Hendriks says 'Take three stones to build our house' but does not mean stones, nor a house – he is talking about the building of a nation by its different peoples. This sort of comparison is called a *metaphor*. You would misunderstand something like this if you did not see that the poet was making a comparison.

Words are also chosen because they cause certain feelings in us. They carry *associations* or *connotations*, apart from the basic meaning they have for us. For instance, when the poet says 'I hear lake water lapping', he reminds us of a relaxed, peaceful feeling. That sentence also shows how poets use the sound of words. If you say and listen to it you will hear the sound to be experienced. Sounds used in rhyming words (e.g. 'instead' and 'unsaid') are, of course, easy to observe. Poets also sometimes choose words whose first syllables begin with similar consonants, as in 'lake' and 'lapping'. That is called *alliteration*.

Some poems have a lot of ideas compressed together and sentences or phrases that have to be unravelled. This has often made people think that poetry is too difficult to read. But you just need to be more careful when the language gets tight, and look carefully at how sentences are built up. Try to work out which noun goes with which verb or what word an adjective describes.

You also have to be a little careful with dialect poems. All over the world there are poets writing very good poems in their local dialect. Since a dialect is a kind of English, if you pay attention you should be able to understand it. Do not assume that these poems are making a joke, or not worthy of as much attention as others.

Neither should you expect that everything a good poem has in it will come to you quickly and easily. Learning to read poems is like learning everything else – it takes time and you have to start with easier ones. But poems are for all of us to enjoy, not just a few of us. Those in this anthology have been chosen to help you to learn to read poems. So don't be afraid. Do what Eve Merriam says in *How to Eat A Poem*. Go ahead. Don't be polite. *Bite In.*

Cecil Gray

To The Teacher

This third edition includes several new poems and *Bite In 3* has been expanded, with the poems now presented in two levels. Students being prepared for the CXC examination have been kept especially in mind in choosing the poems in *Bite In 3*. In particular, Level Two of this book should be found to reflect the preferences of the examiners.

As before, about half of the poems are by Caribbean poets, with the rest covering the whole English-speaking world, plus a few translations.

This symbol indicates that a poem is particularly suitable for choral orchestration.

Cecil Gray has taught for 40 years at primary, secondary and university levels in Trinidad and Jamaica. In 1976 he was awarded the Medal of Merit (Gold – Class 1) of Trinidad & Tobago for 'outstanding and meritorious service in the sphere of Education and Culture'. He retired in 1983 after being Director of an In-Service Diploma in Education programme for nine years at the University of the West Indies. He now spends his time travelling and writing verse.

Acknowledgements

Cecil Gray and the publishers are very grateful to the following
for permission to use the poems which are included in this book:

Marian Reiner for 'How to Eat a Poem' from *Jamboree: Rhymes
for all Times* by Eve Merriam, copyright © 1962, 1964, 1966,
1973, 1984 by Eve Merriam; Martin Carter for 'This is the Dark
Time My Love' from *Selected Poems*; Alfred A. Knopf Inc. for
'Piazza Piece' from Selected Poems by John Crowe Ransom,
Copyright © 1927 by Alfred A. Knopf, Inc. and renewed 1955 by
John Crowe Ransom, reprinted by permission of the publisher;
David Higham Associates for '5 Ways to Kill a Man' by Edwin
Brock, from *5 Ways to Kill a Man*, published by Enitharmon
Press, for 'My Grandmother' by Elizabeth Jennings from
Collected Poems published by Carcanet Press, for 'Absence' by
Elizabeth Jennings from *A Sense of the World*, published by
Andre Deutsch, and for 'The Hand that Signed the Paper' by
Dylan Thomas, from *The Poems* published by J. M. Dent and
Sons Ltd; John McIndoe Printers and Publishers Ltd. for 'Milking
Before Dawn' by Ruth Dallas from *Collected Poems*, published
by University of Otago Press 1987, and for 'Hawk' by Brian
Turner from *Ladders of Rain*, published by John McIndoe, 1978;
Jonathan Clowes Ltd. for 'Lessons' from *A Case of Samples*,
copyright © 1956 Kingsley Amis, reprinted by permission of
Jonathan Clowes Ltd., London on behalf of Kingsley Amis; Miss
R. M. Joseph for 'Baking Day' by Rosemary Joseph; John Johnson
Ltd. for 'Warning' by Jenny Joseph, © Jenny Joseph, from
Selected Poems published by Bloodaxe Books Ltd., 1992; Rogers,
Coleridge and White Ltd. for 'The Lesson' by Edward Lucie-Smith
from *A Tropical Childhood and Other Poems*, and for 'Cold
Beds' by David Sweetman, from *Looking in the Deep End*;
Robson Books Ltd. for 'Silver Wedding' by Vernon Scannell, from
New and Collected Poems; Carcanet Press Ltd. for 'In the Attic'

by Andrew Motion from *The Pleasure Streamers*; Faber and Faber Ltd. for 'Mid-Term Break' and 'Digging' by Seamus Heaney from *Death of a Naturalist*, and for Funeral Rites I by Seamus Heaney from *North*; Vernon Scannell for 'Dead Dog' and 'Incendiary'; Random House UK for 'Airy Hall Isotope', 'Airy Hall's Exits' and 'Airy Hall's Dark Age' by Fred D'Aguiar, from *Airy Hall*; Ian McDonald for 'A Row About the Moon', 'A White Man Considers the Situation' and 'Fuss-pot'; Raymond Barrow for 'Bookmark' and 'There is a Mystic Splendour'; Laurence Pollinger and the Estate of Frieda Lawrence Ravagli for 'Last Lesson of the Afternoon', 'Snake' and 'The Best of School' by D. H. Lawrence; Michael Longley for 'Brothers' from *The Echo Gate*; BIM Magazine, Barbados for 'Beverly is Dead', 'Too Soon it was my Allotted Task', 'Letter to England' and 'The Islander'; Oxford University Press for 'Tom', 'The Emigrants', 'A Slave's Lament on Leaving Home' and 'Masquerader' from *The Arrivants* by Edward Brathwaite.

Although every effort has been made to trace original sources and copyright holders this has not been possible in all cases. The publishers will be pleased to rectify any such omission in future editions.

LEVEL 1

1 Growing Up

A Rain-washed Town By the Sea
Edward Baugh *Jamaica*

The scrunch of the kitchen knife through the long stalks
of ginger lilies I cut for my mother
this leaf-moist morning. Their sharp scent
pierces me.

5   Way above the trumpet
tree, noisy with the gossip of birds,
improbably far, the silver stylus
of a jet chalks the arrow of my
ambition across immaculate blue.

10 Even as I gaze it dissolves in puff balls
of vapour.

              From my school desk, carved
with the names of the lost, the heroes, I shall dream
on the cobalt[1] sea.

15   By mid-day it will rain,
extravagantly, the gutters will gurgle with delight.

These memories define me, I keep them
against that morning when my eyes
no longer turn to greet the sun.

[1] *cobalt* – deep blue

Baking Day
Rosemary Joseph   *England*

Thursday was baking day in our house.
The spicy smell of new baked bread would meet
My nostrils when I came home from school and there would be
Fresh buns for tea, but better still were the holidays.

5 Then I could stay and watch the baking of the bread.
My mother would build up the fire and pull out the damper[1]
Until the flames were flaring under the oven; while it was heating
She would get out her earthenware bowl and baking board.

Into the crater of flour in the bowl she would pour sugar
10 And yeast in hot water; to make sure the yeast was fresh
I had often been sent to fetch it from the grocer that morning,
And it smelt of the earth after rain as it dissolved in the sweet water.

Then her small stubby hands would knead and pummel
The dough until they became two clowns in baggy pantaloons,[2]
15 And the right one, whose three fingers and blue stump
Told of the accident which followed my birth, became whole.

As the hands worked a creamy elastic ball
Took shape and covered by a white cloth was set
On a wooden chair by the fire slowly to rise:
20 To me the most mysterious rite of all.

From time to time I would peep at the living dough
To make sure it was not creeping out of the bowl.
Sometimes I imagined it possessed, filling the whole room,
And we helpless, unable to control its power to grow.

25 But as it heaved above the rim of the bowl mother
Was there, taking it and moulding it into plaited loaves
And buns and giving me a bit to make into a bread man,
With currant eyes, and I, too, was a baker.

My man was baked with the loaves and I would eat him for tea.
30 On Friday night, when the plaited loaves were placed
Under a white napkin on the dining table,
Beside two lighted candles, they became holy.

No bread will ever be so full of the sun as the pieces
We were given to eat after prayers and the cuttings of this bread.
35 My mother, who thought her life had been narrow, did not want
Her daughters to be bakers of bread. I think she was wise.

Yet sometimes, when my cultivated brain chafes[3] at kitchen
Tasks, I remember her, patiently kneading dough
And rolling pastry, her untutored[4] intelligence
40 All bent towards nourishing her children.

[1] *damper* – metal plate to control the fire in the fireplace
[2] *pantaloons* – trousers
[3] *chafes* – feels sore, impatient
[4] *untutored* – unschooled

Ana
Mark McWatt   *Guyana*

While she was yet too young to crawl
my pride would picture her sunlit, outside
playing with flowers
like every poet's child;
5 the frills of her pink dress
waving in the gentlest whim
of her father, observing,
pen in hand, her little gestures
in her world of green.

10 It was a calm and quiet mental scene.

Instead, now,
she leaps at me
off kitchen counters
when my arms and mind are full
15 of other things:

I glimpse the little hands
lunging for my throat,
and in that stiffening split-second
I wish she would miss
20 (serve her damn right)
I pray she won't miss
(little monkey)
but infallibly I feel her hard fingers
her sharp nails
25 in the neutral father-flesh of my neck
and her barbaric howl of delight
stifles my angry shout.
I make to unhorse her with a wild shrug
she thinks it's a game,
'Do that again, Daddy',
30 and like a fool
Daddy does it again.

I've given up the prospect
of pink dresses and flowers;
I let her kick her somersaults
35 off my stomach, hardly noticing now
the muddy footprints on my shirts,
the scratches on my arms . . .
I think I must endure her thorny assaults
precisely because they seem
like self-inflicted wounds.
40

And yet when she is curled in sleep,
like a comma,
I can ponder still the possibility
of finishing all the stanzas
45 with images of her calm beauty
– lying so peaceful on the flower-patterned sheet,
all her brutal fangs of life
retracted behind the closed lids.

My Grandmother
Elizabeth Jennings   *England*

She kept an antique¹ shop – or it kept her.
Among Apostle spoons and Bristol glass,
The faded silks, the heavy furniture,
She watched her own reflection in the brass
5 Salvers² and silver bowls, as if to prove
Polish was all, there was no need of love.

And I remember how I once refused
To go out with her, since I was afraid.
It was perhaps a wish not to be used
10 Like antique objects. Though she never said
That she was hurt, I still could feel the guilt
Of that refusal, guessing how she felt.

Later, too frail to keep a shop, she put
All her best things in one long narrow room
15 The place smelt old, of things too long kept shut,
The smell of absences where shadows come
That can't be polished. There was nothing then
To give her own reflection back again.

And when she died I felt no grief at all,
20 Only the guilt of what I once refused.
I walked into her room among the tall
Sideboards and cupboards – things she never used
But needed: and no finger-marks were there,
Only the new dust falling through the air.

¹ *antique* – old, valuable article
² *salvers* – trays

The Best of School
D.H. Lawrence *England*

The blinds are drawn because of the sun,
And the boys and the room in a colourless gloom
Of underwater float: bright ripples run
Across the walls as the blinds are blown
5 To let the sunlight in; and I,
As I sit on the shores of the class, alone,
Watch the boys in their summer blouses
As they write, their round heads busily bowed:
And one after another rouses
10 His face to look at me,
To ponder very quietly,
As seeing, he does not see.

And then he turns again, with a little, glad
Thrill of his work he turns again from me,
15 Having found what he wanted, having got what was to be had.

And very sweet it is, while the sunlight waves
In the ripening morning, to sit alone with the class
And feel the stream of awakening ripple and pass
From me to the boys, whose brightening souls it laves[1]
20 For this little hour.

This morning, sweet it is
To feel the lads' looks light on me,
Then back in a swift, bright flutter to work:
Each one darting away with his
25 Discovery, like birds that steal and flee.

Touch after touch I feel on me
As their eyes glance at me for the grain
Of rigour[2] they taste delightedly.

As tendrils reach out yearningly,
30 Slowly rotate till they touch the tree

That they cleave unto, and up which they climb
Up to their lives – so they to me.

I feel them cling and cleave to me
As vines going eagerly up; they twine
35 My life with other leaves, my time
Is hidden in theirs, their thrills are mine.

¹ *laves* – bathes, washes
² *rigour* – control, discipline

A Fairy Tale
Anson Gonzalez   *Trinidad and Tobago*

Openly he says: Sir, when I grow up
I want to be a fine man; someone like you.
Secretly he says: You old fool, I'll join
a gang like Applejackers or Navarones
5 and if we catch you in the street
we will break all your bones.
You say you teach me about life
but you don't know that life is strife
between mother and father.

10 Life is nothing to eat when morning comes;
life is no money to buy books and uniforms.
No this, no that, no taking part
in so many things you say make life.
Life is a drunk father on payday,
15 and mother with her feller on Saturday.
Life is sickness and no cash for doctor.
What you teach as life is just a fairy tale.

The Whipping
Robert Hayden   USA

The old woman across the way
    is whipping the boy again
and shouting to the neighbourhood
    her goodness and his wrongs.

5 Wildly he crashes through elephant ears,
    pleads in dusty zinnias,
while she in spite of crippling fat
    pursues and corners him.

She strikes and strikes the shrilly circling
10   boy till the stick breaks
in her hand. His tears are rainy weather
    to woundlike memories:

My head gripped in bony vise
    of knees, the writhing struggle
15 to wrench free, the blows, the fear
    worse than blows that hateful

Words could bring, the face that I
    no longer knew or loved . . .
Well, it is over now, it is over,
20   and the boy sobs in his room,

And the woman leans muttering against
    a tree, exhausted, purged –
avenged in part for lifelong hidings
    she has had to bear.

¹ *hidings* – beatings

Atieno
Marjorie Oludhe-Macgoye   *Nigeria*

Atieno washes dishes,
Atieno plucks the chicken,
Atieno gets up early,
Beds her sack down in the kitchen,
5 Atieno eight years old,
Atieno yo.

Since she is my sister's child
Atieno needs no pay,
While she works my wife can sit
10 Sewing every sunny day:
With her earnings I support
Atieno yo.

Atieno's sly and jealous,
Bad example to the kids
15 Since she minds them, like a schoolgirl
Wants their dresses, shoes and beads,
Atieno yo.

Now my wife has gone to study
Atieno is less free.
20 Don't I keep her, school my own ones,
Pay the party, union fee,
All for progress aren't you grateful
Atieno yo?

Visitors need much attention,
25 All the more when I work night.
That girl spends too long at market.
Who will teach her what is right?
Atieno rising fourteen,
Atieno yo.

₃₀ Atieno's had a baby
So we know that she is bad.
Fifty-fifty it may live
And repeat the life she had
Ending in the post-partum bleeding,
₃₅ Atieno yo.

Atieno's soon replaced.
Meat and sugar more than all
She ate in such a narrow life
Were lavish at her funeral.
₄₀ Atieno's gone to glory,
Atieno yo.

Airy Hall Isotope
Fred D'Aguiar   *Guyana*

Consider our man in a hovel
With no windows, a shack our missiles[1]
Sail through; cracks that do not interrupt
The flow of moonlight or sunlight,
₅ Seen here washing or baking his floor.

Consider too, our woman, reputed to fly
At night on the very broom that sweeps
Her yard printless; the same broom
Used to swipe Dog eyeing Hen's egg,
₁₀ Noisily announced by Hen, drooled over
By Dog that is hungry, hungry;
Dreaming the one dream starring Hen.

Consider last, any boy convalescing[2]
In a house crucified between those two
₁₅ (How he was among the first to fling
Sand stones), spreadeagled
In her mud hut, she massages him
After two days in a pain she alone
Kills with her curious touch.

₂₀ Consider these and you have a life,
Several lives lapping the one sun,
Casting the same lengthening shadows
From a moon so strapping, the children
Play bat and ball and make clean catches.

¹ *missiles* – stones thrown
² *convalescing* – getting over an illness

Coals
Cecil Gray   *Trinidad and Tobago*

My mother cooked in white houses.
His father, I heard, sold coals
somewhere up in the Gonzales
area. I never went there
₅ but at eight we weren't aware
of meanings of symbols like
visiting. He was the brother
I didn't have, a lone friend
that gave joy to the day.
₁₀ His gleaming black skin and my tan
went well together, but better
than everything was the way
we trusted each other when
around us we felt penned
₁₅ in by swarms of gorillas.
We shared all-day laughter,
spoke the same tongue, found
fun in things, not two but one.
Later I learned that
₂₀ he was a coolie, and I a nigger.
And somebody warned me
about getting consumption.
Frowns furrowed my mother's face.
Like satellites that perish in space
₂₅ cut off from earth's station

our transmission suddenly ended.
The cable which had coiled us
together fizzled like coals
that had never ignited,
30 never sparked, never burned.
I didn't know where he went,
he didn't see when I turned.

Dead Dog
Vernon Scannell *England*

One day I found a lost dog in the street.
The hairs about its grin were spiked with blood,
And it lay still as stone. It must have been
A little dog, for though I only stood
5 Nine inches for each one of my four years
I picked it up and took it home. My mother
Squealed, and later father spaded out
A bed and tucked my mongrel down in mud.
I can't remember any feeling but
10 A moderate pity, cool not swollen-eyed;
Almost a godlike feeling now it seems.
My lump of dog was ordinary as bread.
I have no recollection of the school
Where I was taught my terror of the dead.

Discussion and Activities

A Rain-washed Town by the Sea p1

1   'These memories define me' (l 17). Can you think of a word or a phrase that would have the same meaning as 'define' there?
2   A stylus is the hard point of diamond or sapphire that is put to run in the grooves of a record to produce the sound. What comes to mind as an image when you read 'the silver stylus of a jet' (ll 17-18)? What do you suppose the 'I' really means when he says 'it dissolves in puff balls/of vapour' (ll 10-11)?
3   Who do you suppose are 'the lost, the heroes' (l 13)? What is the 'I' doing while at his desk?
4   'I keep them . . . to greet the sun' (ll 17-19). These lines are like an uncovering or disclosure. Of what?
5   Look again at the comparisons or metaphors in lines 8, 10, 16, 17, 18-19, and make whatever comments you can on how well they express what is being said.

Baking Day p2

1   A damper is a metal plate cover used to increase or decrease the flames in a fireplace or oven. When was the oven in the poem used?
2   Why do you think the 'I' used the phrase, 'the living dough' (l 26)? What did she say she imagined could happen? Who or what was 'My man' (l 34)?
3   Pantaloons are wide baggy trousers. What 'became two clowns in baggy pantaloons' (l 19)? Do you find that image a good comparison or metaphor? Say why, or why not.
4   How did 'the right one' (l 20) become 'whole' (l 21)? Why was it not whole before, what had happened to it?
5   'untutored' (l 47) means without much schooling, and 'cultivated' (l 45) means educated, cultured. Who is cultivated? Who untutored? What do you then make of 'chafes at kitchen/Tasks' (ll 45-46)? How did the mother think of her own life? What did she not want for her

daughters? What connection do you make between that and 'my cultivated brain' (l 45)?

6 The words 'white cloth' (l 23), 'rite' (l 25) – a religious practice, 'candles' (l 38), 'holy' (l 38), and 'prayers' (l 40) bring up certain ideas, associations and feelings. Why do you suppose the poet made them belong to the poem?

7 Why could lines 46-48 be said to hold the heart of the poem?

Ana p3

1 How did the speaker imagine the child 'While she was yet too young to crawl' (l 1)? What then makes him say lines 33-34? Look for examples of the child behaving like any other child.

2 Certain things said in the poem are not meant seriously, but are what parents often say out of concern and anxiety. What are they?

3 When the child is asleep, what effect does that have on the 'I'?

4 Two attitudes are interwoven in the poem. Find instances that express each one. Which is the real attitude of the poem, and which the assumed attitude?

My Grandmother p5

1 An antique shop sells things people owned several generations or more ago. Now people pay high prices for them. Which articles in this antique shop are mentioned in the poem?

2 'Only the guilt of what I once refused' (l 20). What did the 'I' refuse? Why? Have you ever felt like that? What is said in line 11 that accounts for 'the guilt'?

3 Where did the grandmother see her reflection? What then do you make of line 6? Is the 'I' saying the grandmother gave more love to polishing things in the shop, or that the 'I' did not have to give love? Say why you come to your conclusion.

The Best of School p6

1 What are the boys (l 1-7) doing? What is the 'I' of the poem doing?

2 What do you see in your imagination from lines 1-5; 8-15; 22-25; 29-35?

3 Explain the comparisons made with these words: 'shores' (l 6); 'stream' (l 18); 'touch after touch' (l 26); 'taste' (l 28).

4 Which lines most clearly give you the attitude and feeling of 'I'?

5   In whatever ways you like, compare this poem of a lesson in the morning with *Last Lesson of the Afternoon* (p20).

A Fairy Tale p7

1   The 'he' says something 'openly' (l 1) and something else 'secretly' (l 3). Which one does he really think? Is he a hypocrite or does he have to be secretive?

2   How is the poem filled with the feeling that the 'he' has inside him?

3   For some people the poem is not a pretty poem. Does that matter? What would you say gives it force and strength?

The Whipping p8

1   What is happening across the road? You know what zinnias are, so what do you think 'elephant ears' (l 5) are?

2   Rain, as you know, brings things back to life. How then would you interpret 'rainy weather to woundlike memories' (ll 11-12)? Does 'my' refer to the boy in line 2 or to someone else? Whose memories are 'woundlike memories'? Memories of what?

3   How can you tell that whippings are referred to, not once, but three times in the poem? 'Well, it is over now, it is over' (l 19)? Could that be referring to more than one of the whippings? If so, which?

4   Why do you think the woman is described as 'purged' (l 22) and 'avenged' (l 23) – having got revenge? What is the meaning then that the poem gives to whippings?

Atieno p9

1   How was Atieno related to the speaker in the poem? Why was she there? What did she have to do in the house? Where did she sleep? What was she given for the work she did? Why did the speaker think she should have been grateful? Why did he say 'Wants their dresses, shoes and beads' (l 16)?

2   'So we know that she is bad' (l 31). Do you agree? Why was she called bad? What is ironic in l 27 in the light of the blame put on her? Do you see any connection between lines 24-25 and line 30? What do you infer from line 34? Why did she have to be 'replaced' (l 36)?

3   Which of these attitudes is revealed in line 36:
    a) impatience; b) haste; c) callousness; d) distress? Point out the irony that lines 37-39 bring out. Having regard to the speaker's

attitude to Atieno would you say line 40 is ironic or not? In what way or ways does Atieno remind you of Cinderella?

1 'missiles' (l 2) are things thrown like stones. Who threw the missiles in the poem? Where did they 'Sail through' (13)?
2 How is it expressed that the moonlight and sunlight easily enter the shack? What do you see 'washing or baking his floor' (l 5)?
3 A woman 'reputed to fly/At night' (ll 6-7) is called an 'old higue' in Guyana and a 'soucouyant' in Trinidad and other islands. Which is 'the same broom' (l 8)?
4 To convalesce is to get better from an illness. Who was 'convalescing' (l 13)? In which house? Who was massaging whom?
5 An isotope is a form of an element. In the poem who seemed to be different from whom? Can you think of how they are alike? What would you imagine the phrase 'crucified between those two' (l 14) is meant to convey? Which are the 'several lives' (l 21)? 'the same lengthening shadows' (l 22)?

1 What do you take 'white houses' (l 1) to mean? Why, do you suppose, was visiting each other's homes referred to as a symbol (l 6)? A symbol of what?
2 Why does the 'I' say 'I learned' (l 19)? Was that something good to learn? Why did he/she not know it before? What does it tell you about the adults around them that they had to grow up among?
3 What is the tone that is meant to come out strongly with the last two lines? a) relief; b) amusement; c) sadness; d) anger. Why do you suppose the poet wrote the poem?

1 Which line in the poem first reveals the dog is dead? How do you know how the boy felt when he saw it? Tell what his parents did.
2 What feelings was the boy aware of at the burial of the dog? Did he feel fear of the dead dog at any time?
3 How do you interpret the word 'school' (l 13)? Which of these attitudes is the poem expressing? a) fear of dead people and animals; b) rejection of things children learn; c) disgust for stray dogs?

2 Conflicts and Crises

A Row About the Moon
Ian McDonald   *Trinidad and Tobago*

Regular as religion, every month,
There is a row about the moon.

When the full moon comes to flower
It floods the earth with silver colour.
5 A basin of white water spills and froths
And slops over all the town.
A bright pallor[1] spreads in dark corridors.

Some in Mercy Ward complain:
They hate and fear the great white ghost
10 That makes them think of Jumbie-birds.
They want the tall blinds pulled across:
Keep out the coffin-colour, these ones say,
Keep out the leper-shine,
This fungus-staining of our skin.

15 Some want the moon let in:
They like the pallid beauty everywhere,
The waxen light of lilies that it throws.
Throw the windows wide and let her in,
The grey fox of the night, our pet,
20 We may not see again, so sleek, so silvery,
Let her in!

[1] *pallor* – paleness

A Tale of Two Tongues
Earl McKenzie *Jamaica*

Miss Ida speaks only English to God.
Scholars cannot fault the diction
of her graces and prayers;
to her, it is the language of holy things;
5 and the giver of commandments
deserves a grammar of respectability
as firm and as polished
as his tablets of stone.

But to fellow mortals she speaks Creole,
10 the tongue of the markets and the fields,
the language of labrish,
su-su, proverbs and stories,
hot-words, tracings and preckeh;
it is the way to get
15 hard-ears pickney to listen
and facety men to keep off;
it is the tongue of belly laughs
and sweet body action.

And to Miss Ida it is no bother
20 to laugh and suffer in one language
and worship in another.

In the New World
Elaine Terranova *USA*

There is my uncle
pulling the new Dodge to the side
of the road, first in a family
of ox drivers to drive a car.
5 He is a farmer. It is
the only living thing he knows
how to exact from this new earth.

He is taking his corn and eggs
to market over clear, paved road.

10 Next to him, my aunt
in a checkered housedress
peers out through the same
wide window. Their daughter
is in back, the bright
15 sixteen-year-old they dote on,
an American. My uncle and aunt
are thin and grey as dust,
They have poured all their colour
into her: red health, the grain shade
20 of her hair, green eyes
open to all they can contain.

What had happened
is a flat tyre, some puncture
of the usual. My uncle
25 will jack up the ton of metal
with his own strength
and clever new tools. He is
an upright man, student of God
all his days. Everything waits
30 for him to hold it up. Behind them
someone doesn't see my uncle
pull up along the curve.
Suddenly, nothing will take them
any further. The child is dead,
35 the farm lost. The woman
must walk in pain all her life.
For years my uncle sits
more still than anyone,
hands locked between his knees.

The Lesson
Edward Lucie-Smith   *Jamaica*

'Your father's gone,' my bald headmaster said.
His shiny dome and brown tobacco jar
Splintered at once in tears. It wasn't grief.
I cried for knowledge which was bitterer
5 Than any grief. For there and then I knew
That grief has uses – that a father dead
Could bind the bully's fist a week or two;
And then I cried for shame, then for relief.

I was a month past ten when I learnt this:
10 I still remember how the noise was stilled
In school-assembly when my grief came in.
Some goldfish In a bowl quietly sculled
Around their shining prison on its shelf.
They were indifferent. All the other eyes
15 Were turned towards me. Somewhere in myself
Pride, like a goldfish, flashed a sudden fin.

Last Lesson of the Afternoon
D.H. Lawrence   *England*

When will the bell ring, and end this weariness?
How long have they tugged the leash, and strained apart
My pack of unruly hounds! I cannot start
Them again on a quarry of knowledge they hate to hunt,
5 I can haul them and urge them no more.

No longer now can I endure the brunt
Of the books that lie out on the desks; a full threescore
Of several insults of blotted pages, and scrawl
Of slovenly work that they have offered me,
10 I am sick, and what on earth is the good of it all?
What good to them or me, I cannot see!

So, shall I take
My last dear fuel of life to heap on my soul
And kindle my will to a flame that shall consume
15 Their dross[1] of indifference; and take the toll
Of their insults in punishment? – I will not! –

I will not waste my soul and my strength for this.
What do I care for all that they do amiss![2]
What is the point of this teaching of mine, and of this
20 Learning of theirs? It all goes down the same abyss.

What does it matter to me, if they can write
A description of a dog, or if they can't?
What is the point? To us both, it is all my aunt!
And yet I'm supposed to care, with all my might,
25 I do not, and will not; they won't and they don't; and that's all!
I shall keep my strength for myself; they can keep theirs as well.
Why should we beat our heads against the wall
Of each other? I shall sit and wait for the bell.

[1] *dross* – trash, waste
[2] *amiss* – wrong

Warning
Jenny Joseph   *England*

When I am an old woman I shall wear purple
With a red hat which doesn't go, and doesn't suit me,
And I shall spend my pension on brandy and summer gloves
And satin sandals, and say we've no money for butter.
5 I shall sit down on the pavement when I'm tired
And gobble up samples in shops and press alarm bells
And run my stick along the public railings
And make up for the sobriety[1] of my youth.
I shall go out in my slippers in the rain
10 And pick the flowers in other people's gardens
And learn to spit.

You can wear terrible shirts and grow more fat
And eat three pounds of sausages at a go
Or only bread and pickle for a week
15 And hoard pens and pencils and beermats and things in boxes.

But now we must have clothes that keep us dry
And pay our rent and not swear in the street
And set a good example for the children.
We will have friends to dinner and read the papers.

20 But maybe I ought to practise a little now?
So people who know me are not too shocked and surprised
When suddenly I am old and start to wear purple.

1 *sobriety* – carefulness, soberness

The Batterer
Fleur Adcock *New Zealand*

What can I have done to earn
the Batterer striding here beside me,
checking up with his blue-china
sidelong eyes that I've not been bad –

5 not glanced across the street, forgetting
to concentrate on what he's saying;
not looked happy without permission,
or used the wrong form of his name?

How did he get here, out of the past,
10 with his bulging veins and stringy tendons,
fists clenched, jaw gritted,
about to burst with babble and rage?

Did I elect him? Did I fall
asleep and vote him in again?
15 Yes, that'll be what he is: a nightmare;
but someone else's now, not mine.

Snake
D.H. Lawrence   *England*

A snake came to my water-trough
On a hot, hot day, and I in pyjamas for the heat,
To drink there.
In the deep, strange-scented shade of the great dark
    carob-tree
5 I came down the steps with my pitcher
And must wait, must stand and wait, for there
      he was at the trough before me.
He reached down from a fissure[1] in the earth-wall
    in the gloom
And trailed his yellow-brown slackness soft-bellied down,
    over the edge of the stone trough
And rested his throat upon the stone bottom,
10 And where the water had dripped from the tap,
    in a small clearness,
He sipped with his straight mouth,
Softly drank through his straight gums, into his
    slack long body.
Silently.

Someone was before me at my water-trough,
15 And I, like a second comer, waiting
He lifted his head from his drinking, as cattle do,
And looked at me vaguely, as drinking cattle do,
And flickered his two-forked tongue from his lips,
    and mused a moment,
And stooped and drank a little more,
20 Being earth-brown, earth-golden from the burning,
    bowels of the earth,
On the day of Sicilian July, with Etna smoking.

The voice of my education said to me
He must be killed,
For in Sicily the black, black snakes are innocent,
    the gold are venomous.

25 And voices in me said, if you were a man
You would take a stick and break him now,
        and finish him off.

But must I confess how I liked him,
How glad I was he had come like a guest in quiet,
        to drink at my water-trough
And depart peacefully, pacified, and thankless,
30 Into the burning bowels of this earth.

Was it cowardice, that I dared not kill him?
Was it perversity,[2] that I longed to talk to him?
Was it humility, to feel so honoured?
I felt so honoured.

35 And yet those voices:
"If you were not afraid, you would kill him!"

And truly I was afraid, I was most afraid,
But even so, honoured still more
That he should seek my hospitality
40 From out the dark door of the secret earth.

He drank enough
And lifted his head, dreamily, as one who had drunken,
And flickered his tongue like a forked night on the air,
        so black,
Seeming to lick his lips,
45 And looked around like a god, unseeing, into the air,
And slowly turned his head,
And slowly, very slowly, as if thrice adream,
Proceeded to draw his slow length curving round
And climb again the broken bank of my wall-face.

50 And as he put his head into that dreadful hole,
And as he slowly drew up, snake-easing his shoulders,
        and entered farther,
A sort of horror, a sort of protest against his
        withdrawing into that horrid black hole,
Deliberately going into the blackness, and slowly

    drawing himself after,
Overcame me now his back was turned.

55 I looked round, I put down my pitcher,
    I picked up a clumsy log
    And threw it at the water-trough with a clatter.

    I think it did not hit him,
    But suddenly that part of him that was left behind
        convulsed in undignified haste,

60 Writhed like lightning, and was gone
    Into the black hole, the earth-lipped fissure in the
        wall-front,
    At which, in the intense still noon; I stared with fascination.

    And immediately I regretted it.
    I thought how paltry,[3] how vulgar, what a mean act!
65 I despised myself and the voices of my accursed
        human education.

    And I thought of the albatross,[4]
    And I wished he would come back, my snake.

    For he seemed to me again like a king,
    Like a king in exile, uncrowned in the underworld,
70 Now due to be crowned again.

    And so, I missed my chance with one of the lords
    Of life.
    And I have something to expiate;[5]
    A pettiness.

[1] *pacified* – satisfied
[2] *perversity* – wilful disobedience
[3] *paltry* – petty, insignificant
[4] *albatross* – a large sea bird. Killing an albatross is believed to bring bad luck.
[5] *expiate* – pay for

Mother Jackson Murders the Moon
Gloria Escoffery *Jamaica*

Mother Jackson
sees the moon coming at her
and slams the door of her shack
so hard
5 the tin louvres shudder with eagerness
to let the moon in.
If she should cry for help
the dog would skin his teeth at her,
the cat would hoist his tail
10 and pin the moonlit sky
to the gutter;
the neighbours would maybe
douse her in chicken's blood
and hang her skin to dry
15 on the packy tree.
Mother Jackson
swallows her bile and sprinkles oil
from the kitchen bitch
on her ragged mattress.
20 Then she lights a firestick and waits
for the moon to come in and take her.

Discussion and Activities

A Row About the Moon p17

1 This poem comes from a collection called *Mercy Ward*, all about patients in a hospital ward. When do they have a row? Why?

2 'Jumbie birds' (l 10) are owls, which some people believe bring death. Why do the complainers remember them? How do they describe the moonlight?

3 Why do you think some say 'our pet/We may never see again' (ll 19-20)? How do those think of the moonlight?

4 As what figure of speech is the word 'flower' (l 3) used? Describe the imagery (pictures) put into the poem in lines 4-7. Which is more important in the poem, story or imagery?

A Tale of Two Tongues p18

1 'Creole' (l 9) refers to a dialect of English. How are you told Miss Ida has a perfect command of English? What does she find has 'respectability' (l 6)? How are 'tablets of stone' (l 8) and 'commandments' (l 5) related? What do you imagine she would think of someone who said prayers in 'Creole'?

2 To whom does Miss Ida speak 'Creole'? 'tracings' (l 13) are words of abuse about someone and his/her family; 'labrish' is gossip. If you are not a Jamaican try to imagine the kind of situation the words 'su-su' and 'preckeh' are used in. Who do you think are called 'hard-ears pickney' (l 15)? 'Facety' is a Jamaican word for feisty, meaning aggressive, bold. How do you imagine the 'facety men' (l 16) behave? How does Miss Ida deal with the conflict some people have about speaking a dialect?

3 In what figurative way is the phrase 'as firm and as polished' (l 7) used? Would you agree that the word 'tongue' is used metaphorically, or not? Say why.

In the New World p18

1 America, as you know, was called The New World. Where would you say the poem is set? Why then does the speaker refer to the place as 'this new earth' (l 7)? Why do you suppose the Dodge car was new (l 2)? What was it being used for? Who were in it? Why did the Uncle have to use tools (l 27)? How do you

interpret line 33? How does the term 'new world' fit in with the uncle and aunt?

2 Why do you suppose it had to be explained that the daughter was 'an American' (l 16)? Which lines show the importance of the daughter to the lives of the uncle and aunt? What does line 34 tell you about her? Which two meanings are there in 'Suddenly, nothing will take them any further' (ll 33-34)? 'the farm lost' (l 35). Can you imagine why? How were their lives changed?

3 Consider which one of these feelings or attitudes is strongest in the poem and say why you think so: disappointment, shame, pathos, annoyance. Do you think the simplicity of the poem emphasises the tragedy enough or should the poet have used stronger language?

The Lesson p20

1 In the first line the headmaster gives the 'I' of the poem some news. Why would you infer the school was a boarding school where students also lived? What 'Splintered' (l 3)? How did that happen? 'It wasn't grief' (l 3). What then brought tears? What was the 'knowledge' referred to in line 4? Why do you suppose that the 'I' then 'cried for shame' (l 8)? Shame about what?

2 How do you understand 'when my grief came in' (l 11)? 'the noise was stilled' (l 10). Where? Why? What eyes 'Were turned towards me' (l 15)? Why were the goldfish the only ones who were indifferent? When did the 'I' feel pride? What caused it to rise somewhere in himself?

3 Usually someone cries for grief on the death of his or her father. What was the relief the 'I' cried for? Could there be some reason why love for his father took second place? Why do you suppose the poem was named 'The Lesson'?

4 The headmaster's head is called a 'shiny dome' (l 2), as a boy might say. Why that particular comparison? Which of these words are also used metaphorically a) splintered (l 3); b) bitterer (l 4); c) grief (l 6); d) bind (l 7); e) stilled (l 10); f) grief (l 11); g) goldfish (l 12); h) sculled (l 12); i) prison (l 13); j) shelf (l 13); k) flashed (l 16); l) fin (l 16). In each case where a word is used as a metaphor try to point out the comparison the poet is making. Choose two metaphors which you think are very good comparisons and say why you think so.

Last Lesson of the Afternoon p20

1 What are the 'pack of unruly hounds' (l 3) doing?
2 What attitude of the teacher are you aware of in the first five lines? Does concern or worry come into it? What makes you say so?
3 What seems to come out as the teacher's attitude at the end that you didn't expect at the beginning? What appears to indicate that attitude?
4 Does the poet mean that the teacher really believes line 25, or is he expressing a temporary mood? How can you tell?
5 What are called 'insults' (l 8)? Why? How deeply is it meant?
6 Which one or more of these would you call the poem:
   a) a humorous story meant as a joke; b) bitter and angry;
   c) an honest, sincere expression of real experience. Say why.

Warning p21

1 'sobriety' (l 8) is good, normal behaviour as society expects. Why do you suppose the 'I' wants to 'make up for the sobriety' (l 8) of her youth? In what ways does she think she ought to do it?
2 What is the behaviour expected of her now? How seriously do you take the line 'But maybe I ought to practise a little now' (l 20)? How seriously do you take the whole poem?
3 Find as many touches of humour as you can in the poem and discuss them.

The Batterer p22

1 To batter someone is to beat or mistreat him/her. Describe the appearance of the batterer as the 'I' saw him. Which lines tell the offences for which the 'I' was battered?
2 What do 'out of the past' (l 9), 'fall asleep' (ll 13-14), and 'nightmare' (l 15) tell you? Why do you suppose the batterer is 'someone else's' (l 16) nightmare now?
3 What feeling would you say the poem is charged with? Give evidence in it to support your opinion.

Snake p23

1 What early clues indicate the kind of country it is? When do you actually learn which country it is?
2 What are people's usual attitudes to snakes? What does 'The voice

of my education' (l 23) have to do with that attitude? What is the first sign you meet of the poet's attitude of respect and admiration? Pick out all other signs – words, phrases, etc., – which help to signal his attitude.

3 What images do you see from lines 7-13; 16-21; 42-49; 58-60?

4 Do the last four lines tell you that the 'I' felt shame, regret, anger, fear, disgust, excitement or what?

5 In a famous poem by S.T. Coleridge called *The Rime of the Ancient Mariner*, bad luck is brought on a ship by a sailor who kills an albatross (a large sea bird). Why did the 'I' in *Snake* think of the albatross?

6 What makes this poem memorable, i.e. very interesting and impressive, although it has no rhymes, no regular rhythm, and has a tone of ordinary conversation? Does the 'conversational' tone add something to the effect of the poem? If so, try to say what.

Mother Jackson Murders the Moon p26

1 What is Mother Jackson imagining about the moon? What does that tell you about her? What does she imagine in lines 7-15?

2 'The kitchen bitch' (l 16) is a lamp. Why do you suppose she sprinkles oil from it? 'and waits' (l 20). What do you imagine happens after 'and waits'? Why do you think the poet tells no more?

3 Would you say the poem is a comic poem or a tragic poem? Give your reason or reasons.

4 How well would you say the poet got into the mind of Mother Jackson? Give evidence for your opinion. How did that help you or hinder you in experiencing the poem?

3 Struggle and Survival

Memories of a Grasscutter
Rajandaye Ramkissoon-Chen   *Trinidad and Tobago*

Head tied with rags of cloth
Bare-backed with sweat-shine
Beneath the sun –
That's how my father toiled
5 My father's father, and his
Cutlassing with the dance of twigs
To the music of the wind,
And beneath the open sky they lay
Counting its jewels for their wealth.
10 Now, like that old palm-tree stooped
With leaves with withered brown
I long
To hear again the cutlass sounds –
Swish on grass
15 Knock on root-wood
Clang on vagrant stone
In the fields,
As I lean on the 'crook'd stick'
With the figure-head of my toil.

Just a Passer-By
Oswald Mbuyiseni Mtsaali   *South Africa*

I saw them clobber him with kieries.
I heard him scream with pain
like a victim of slaughter;
I smelt fresh blood gush
5 from his nostrils.
and flow on the street.

I walked into the church
and knelt in the pew
"Lord! I love you,
10 I also love my neighbour. Amen."

I came out
my heart as light as an angel's kiss
on the cheek of a saintly soul.

Back home I strutted
15 past a crowd of onlookers.
Then she came in –
my woman neighbour:
"Have you heard? They've killed your brother."
"O! No! I heard nothing. I've been to church."

George
Dudley Randall   *USA*

When I was a boy desiring the title of man
And toiling to earn it
In the inferno[1] of the foundry knockout,
I watched and admired you working by my side,
5 As goggled, with mask on your mouth and shoulders
        bright with sweat,
You mastered the monstrous, lumpish cylinder blocks,
And when they clotted the line and plunged to the floor
With force enough to tear your foot in two,
You calmly stepped aside.

10 One day when the line broke down and the blocks reared up
Groaning, grinding, and mounted like an ocean wave
And then rushed thundering down like an avalanche,
And we frantically dodged, then braced our heads together
To form an arch to lift and stack them,
15 You gave me your highest accolade:[2]
You said: "You not afraid of sweat. You strong as a mule."

Now, here, in the hospital,
In a ward where old men wait to die,
You sit, and watch time go by.
20 You cannot read the books I bring, not even

32

Those that are only picture books,
As you sit among the senile wrecks,
The psychopaths, the incontinent.

One day when you fell from your chair and stared at
    the air
25 With the look of fright which sight of death inspires,
I lifted you like a cylinder block, and said,
'Don't be afraid
Of a little fall, for you'll be here
A long time yet, because you're strong as a mule.'

1 *inferno* – raging fire
2 *accolade* – promise
3 *senile* – weak and helpless with age

The Coming
Tony Matthews   *Jamaica*

A small slice of sun
illuminates what may well be, for them,
the final run.
A scratchy, metallic voice
5 claws the evening air:

'Will all the passengers
for BOAC Flight 808,
Kingston to London *via* New York,
please board the plane.
10 Thank you.'

Final hugs, last kisses.
Unashamed, wet eyes.
Brightly-coloured dresses.
Ill-fitting, new shoes,
15 Large, Sunday-best trousers,
flapping in the breeze.
Old ladies, shifting corsets
for that little ease.

The engines come to life
20 with a deafening roar.
Now, only a dot of silver
can be seen, as the huge metal cage swings
high into the sky
towards THE PROMISED, HELPING HAND.

25 Slowly, we turn away
to Kingston, to face the future
without the ones in the sky.

We know there's something
coming to take us away, too.

St Ann Saturday
Christine Craig   *Jamaica*

Saturday afternoon. So many shades
of black swinging down the road.
funeral time.
Nice afternoon she get eh!

5 If.

An so many smaddy¹ turn out
like a ole days funeral

Dats right.

Imagine her time come
10 so quick. Well de Lord giveth
an de Lord taketh away.

Sure ting.

Children walk lightly, plaits
floating with rainbows of ribbons

15 beside auntie's strong hips, uncle's
suit so dark his body is held in tight,
moves only back, front, front, back.
Auntie's hips roll sedately, heave
like waves beside the dancing plaits.

20 You see her big daughter come from
Canada. Me no like how she look
at all. No sir. She look a way.
Me never memba say she look so mawga.[2]
Me mind tell me she catching
hard time over dere.
25 Imagine is six pickney Miss Martha
raise, she one bring dem up an
send dem out into de world.
Six pickney, she one.
30 Well as I say she send dem
out an is one degge, degge
daughta come home fe bury her.

Still an all, dem neva come
when she was hearty, no mek sense
35 dem come when she direckly dead.

A dat too.

Starapple leaves, double toned
bend quiet over the steady walking,
walking for Miss Martha gone to rest.
40 The path she walked, food to market
children to school, Sunday to Church,
steady walking. In the end, alone
under the starapple leaves a hush
fell over her, silence of age
45 of no names left to call
to table. Of no news from
Delroy or Maisie or Petal
or Lennie or Edith or Steve.

Nice turn out Miss Martha have.
50 See Mass Len clear from Topside.
An no Granny Bailey dat from Retreat?
Well I neva. Tink seh she dead
long time. Time passing chile
we all moving down de line.

¹ *smaddy* – persons
² *mawga* – meagre, thin

Telephone Conversation
Wole Soyinka *Nigeria*

The price seemed reasonable, location
Indifferent. The landlady swore she lived
Off premises. Nothing remained
But self-confession. "Madam," I warned,
5 "I hate a wasted journey – I am – African."
Silence. Silenced transmission of
Pressurised good-breeding. Voice, when it came,
Lip-stick coated, long gold-rolled
Cigarette-holder pipped. Caught I was, foully.

10 "HOW DARK?" . . . I had not misheard . . . "ARE YOU LIGHT
OR VERY DARK?" Button B. Button A. Stench
Of rancid breath of public-hide-and-speak.
Red booth. Red pillar-box. Red double-tiered
Omnibus squelching tar. It *was* real! Shamed
15 By ill-mannered silence, surrender
Pushed dumbfoundment to beg simplification
Considerate she was, varying the emphasis –
"ARE YOU DARK? OR VERY LIGHT?" Revelation came.
"You mean – like plain or milk chocolate?"
20 Her assent was clinical, crushing in its light
Impersonality. Rapidly, wave-length adjusted,
I chose, "West African sepia" – and as an afterthought,

"Down in my passport." Silence for spectroscopic
Flight of fancy, till truthfulness clanged her accent
25 Hard on the mouthpiece. "WHAT'S THAT?" conceding[1]
"DON'T KNOW WHAT THAT IS." "Like brunette."
"THAT'S DARK, ISN'T IT?" "Not altogether.
Facially, I am brunette, but madam, you should see
The rest of me. Palm of my hand, soles of my feet
30 Are a peroxide blonde. Friction, caused –
Foolishly madam – by sitting down, has turned
My bottom raven black – One moment madam!" – sensing
Her receiver rearing on the thunderclap
About my ears – "Madam," I pleaded, "Wouldn't you rather
35 See for yourself?"

[1] *conceding* – admitting

Pundit
Selwyn Bhajan   *Guyana*

A cold mud wall, a bed on bags on boards,
His house.
Sudama sits upon the cow-dung pasted floor
And chants a morning Puja[1] before the milking of the cow.

5 A village, folded in the fist of forest
Wakes.
The cutlass sack laced on his back
Poor coolie,[2] barefooted like his father was,
And children are,
10 Makes the cocoa land.
Poor coolie's wife.
The bake in sack, laced on her back,
Trods lightly steps behind.

Slow muted toil.
15 Slow stubborn sweat.
A break for bake.

Slow muted toil, there is more joy in death.
And then, again sun dies.
Again the corn-birds have been nested.
20 Again with night, their chants, slow rise,
The Puja has begun.

Come sad chants, return,
Refresh a longing mind,
Sudama's voice must break this evening's cold,
25 The Cutya's[3] smell of mud and ash,
The brass,
The turn of moth-tongued pages
Heavy with the grease of fingers
Searching after Sanscrit[4] hymns.

30 Return childhood's evenings,
Lend me coolie voices oiled with cocoa sweat,
Let me hear again a Pundit's yearn,
There is much solace in those dry throats.

[1] *Puja* – a prayer or rite
[2] *coolie* – a labourer in S.E. Asia
[4] *Cutya's* – a hut for prayers
[5] *Sanscrit* – ancient language of India

A Slave's Lament on Leaving Home
Edward Brathwaite   *Barbados*

It will be a long long time before we see
this land again, these trees
again, drifting inland with the sound
of surf, smoke rising
5 It will be a long time before we see
these farms again, soft wet slow green
again: Aburi, Akwamu,
mist rising

Watch now these hard men, cold
10 clear eye'd like the water we ride,
skilful with sail and the rope and the tackle.[1]

Watch now these cold men, bold
as the water banging the bow in a sudden wild tide,
indifferent, it seems, to the battle
15   of wind in the water;
for our blood, mixed
soon with their passion in sport,

in indifference, in anger,
will create new soils, new souls, new
20   ancestors; will flow like this tide fixed

to the star by which this ship floats
to new world, new waters, new
harbours, the pride of our ancestors mixed

with the wind and the water
25   the flesh and the flies, the whips and the fixed
fear of pain in this chained and welcoming port.

¹ *tackle* – for rigging sails

Father
Rajandaye Ramkissoon-Chen   *Trinidad and Tobago*

Daylight cranked the start of work.
The ricemill throbbed with life
And,
My father's mind rolled
5   With the mill's flat belt.

His measure was the pitch-oil-tin.
Each one, paddy-filled
My father heaved in-
to the mill's high funnel.

39

10 The milled rice, white,
   Ran down the spout
   Like the stitches on his kurtah¹ hem,
   Yellow paddy shells converting
   To gold studs for its neck.

15 Beneath the house
   Was the depository for husk.
   We piled hillocks
   Wide
   And to the flooring top.
20 With buckets in hand
   Like little Hillarys we climbed.
   We dug footprints
   Into savings
   For the arid times.

25 I once sold rice husk
   The jute bags grew
   Over my head
   I pressed my mind
   Like a calculator
30 And displayed the figures
   In pennies and cents.

   The muffler once snorted
   Sparks and smoke
   Over dried-leaf eddies
35 Little brass-plated
   Doing a Hindu *aarti.*

   A pitchyard thrust back
   Our home.
   Paddy dried like nuggets
40 In the sun.
   Animals standing
   And awaiting their loads
   splashed in the yard
   Bullion-lumps of dung.

45 Raleigh, here,
Would have found together
Both his La Brea and
The City of Manoa.

¹ *kartah* – a tunic worn by Hindus

Sunday in the Lane
Christine Craig *Jamaica*

Every Sunday in the lane
church heavies the gentle air.
Every Sunday in the lane
someone beats a child.
5 Over the syrup of Praise the Lord
comes a cry, sobs tearing across
the yards and dusty trees.

Every Saturday in the lane
comes the rub a dub of sounds.
10 Reggae, Motown, a giant broom
to sweep away the week's worries.
The clothes that can't wash for the
tap's dry. The rent that can't pay
for the money no nuff. The man
15 that swearing you down sake of he
have a little young gal on de side.

Comes Sunday, smoke of burning
rubbish starts the morning. Dirt
all banished before a whiff, a
20 teasing hint of Sunday dinner
can find its spicy liberation. A lull
then the Lord comes down in radio glory
and someone beats a child.
Chastisement and Church, Sunday brothers
25 in the lane.

Contre Jour
Elizabeth Bartlett *England*

Contre Jour, he said, a photographic phrase,
literally against the day, I suppose.
I'll put a little by, my mother would say,
against the day when we have nothing left.
5 Limp purse, well-rubbed, false teeth
not quite fitting, second-hand clothes,
knees like nutmeg graters. Whatever happened
to those gentle scented mothers sitting in gardens
under a shady hat, the maid mincing across the grass
10 with a tray for afternoon tea in early June?
It was never summer for her. It didn't reach
the dank back yard, the airless little rooms,
where the kitchen range brought a flush
to her face as she perpetually bent over it,
15 cooking, ironing, shifting sooty kettles round,
but never posed for her husband to catch
the tilt of her head against the day,
who never owned a camera anyway.

My inner lens clicks faster, faster
20 contre jour, for now her face is fading
as her life recedes. You must have known
that once she minced across the lawn
carrying a loaded tray for mothers
like yours, whose photographs have
25 frames of silver, like the ones
she polished every week for twelve
pounds per annum and her keep.

Charity
Connie Bensley   *England*

Trouble has done her good,
Trouble has stopped her trivializing everything,
Giggling too much,
Glittering after other people's husbands.

5 Trouble has made her think;
Taken her down a peg,
Knocked the stuffing out of her.
Trouble has toned down the vulgarity.
Under the bruises she looks more deserving:
10 Someone you'd be glad to throw a rope to,
Somewhere to send your old blouses,
Or those wormy little windfalls.

Flint
Earl McKenzie   *Jamaica*

The day after the rain,
during the retaliation of the sun,
the land broke.

Yam
5 potato
and cassava
fields

slid
down
10 the hillside.

Birds and butterflies flew into the air.

Earthworms, frogs and mongooses
mingled with colliding flint stones.

Sparks struck dry guava leaves,
15 darted into tossing guinea grass.
And when the land was still again

the flames spread out,
climbed vines into bamboo groves,
ran along branches into cane fields,
20 and proclaimed their conquest from the tops of trees.

Later in the village people cried
and searched their lives for sins.
And in the night
the sounds of their singing and drumming
25 were blown by the wind
across the moonlit fields
of ashes and dust.

Hawk

Brian Turner *New Zealand*

The hawk is alone
in the ownerless sky.
He glides over fields
and soars above the hills:
5 believe me, he will sell

his supremacy dear. The
casual ease of his flight
deceives the uninitiated:
that haughty, languidly[1]
10 sweeping hook-nosed bird

spells threat, death. He
is prying Director,[2]
is the smarmy Al Capone[3]
of the air; the shushing wing-beat
15 harbours the sound

of cruising limousines. All
that tremble tremble with just
fear for he does not
intend to stay long
20 up there alone in the air . . .

No hawk is real hawk
without hot blood
besmirching his beak, without
flesh gripped between his sharp
25 God-given claws of his feet.

[1] *languidly* – lazily
[2] *Director* – head of the CIA, American spies
[3] *Al Capone* – A Chicago gangster in the 1930s

Discussion and Activities

1 The profession of medicine has a symbol of a stick with a
figurehead of a serpent. Could that be the 'crook'd stick'/With the
figurehead of my toil' (ll 18-19)? If so, what is the toil of the 'I' in
the poem? Why do you suppose the 'I' longs 'To hear again the
cutlass sounds' (l 13)? If the 'I' is a doctor, what has happened since
he/she used to hear them?

2 What jewels did the 'I's foreparents court for their wealth? How do
you interpret 'the dance of twigs/To the music of the wind' (ll 16-
17)? What does that phrase sound like when you read it aloud? Has
the poet used onomatopoeia there? (Onomatopoeia is the
resemblance of the sound of words to what the words are telling
about.) Is there onomatopoeia anywhere else in the poem?

3 The words 'dance' (l 6), 'music' (l 7), 'jewels' (l 9), and 'vagrant'
(l 16) are used as metaphors. Give an opinion on each one with
respect to how well it helps a reader to get the idea that must be
imagined.

4 Discuss any similarities you find between this poem and *Pundit*
(p37)

1 This imagined incident takes place in South Africa, where for
generations black people had no rights, and were treated unjustly.
What did the 'I' in the poem actually see happen?

2 Why, would you say, did the 'I' go into the church? How did he or
she answer the neighbour? Can you suggest why he or she behaved
that way?

3 Do you think 'brother' (l 18) could mean someone not related to the
speaker? If so, what is being suggested about the behaviour of the
speaker? Do you think the poet is being sarcastic about people who
pretend to be pious Christians, or is he just showing how people are
forced to behave under an oppressive system? See whether there is
anything in the poem to help you make up your mind.

1 An accolade is a reward like a medal or ribbon for outstanding

service or performance. What 'accolade' (l 19) did George give the
'I' in the poem? Why?

2   Where is George now? Who are referred to as 'senile wrecks' (l 26)?
As 'psychopaths' (l 27)? Why do you suppose George fell from his
chair? (l 28)? How did the 'I' repay George with an accolade?

3   In what sense is the whole poem an accolade, a praise-poem?

The Coming p33

1   How soon do you realise that people are about to board a plane?
Where is it going to? Where are the people leaving from?

2   What impressions do you get of the people about to leave?

3   What does line 24 tell you about why they are leaving? In what way
could the flight be 'the final run' (l 3) for them? Who is the poem
about, those leaving or those left?

St Ann Saturday p34

1   Which two meanings could you give to 'shades of black' How
popular and well-liked would you say Miss Martha was?

2   How can you tell more than one person is speaking in the poem? Is
the person speaking lines 37-48 one of those speaking in lines 4-36
and in lines 49-54? Who speaks lines 1-3?

3   Describe the life Miss Martha lived as outlined in lines
40-48. If she was well-liked in her community, how do you
account for the attitude of five of her children? Did Miss Martha
deserve their negligence? How does 'in the end, alone' (l 42) make
you feel?

4   What do you imagine was the intention of the poet in writing this
poem? Do you think the poet should have used stronger and more
dramatic words to bring out our sympathy for Miss Martha, or do the
simple words and language serve the purpose better? Why do you
suppose the starapple leaves are described (ll 37-38)? How do lines
37-48 serve to bring out a hush and silence after the conversation
before? How does the hush, the silence, help to solemnise Miss
Martha's funeral? On what kind of note does the poem end in 'Time
passing chile we all moving down de line' (ll 53-54)?

1 Three clues – 'price' (l 1), 'location' (l 1) and 'landlady' (1-2) are present at the very beginning. What was the telephone conversation about? Who were the people speaking?

2 By lines 3-4 'nothing remained/But self-confession'. What does *nothing remained* tell you? What do you think was said in the conversation before what was reported in the poem? What did one speaker think had to be 'confessed'? Why? What questions did the landlady ask then? Why has the poet put 'was' (l 14) in italics? How do you think the conversation ended, considering what is said in lines 32-34?

3 What do you take 'good-breeding' (l 7) to mean? What symbols of good breeding are mentioned? Why has the poet used *pressurised* here?

4 The telephone booth is described as a 'public hide-and-speak' (l 12). Where else does the poet use comparison? Say what you get from each comparison you find.

5 Using only what is said or suggested in the poem what do you judge to be the poet's purpose in writing the poem? Why do you say so?

1 The word 'coolie' is regarded by some people in Trinidad as offensive. It means a labourer or carrier of loads. Why does the speaker in the poem say "Poor coolie" (ll 8 and 11)? What do you imagine as 'Slow muted toil' (l 14)? Why do you think the phrase is repeated? To whom are the chants asked to 'return'? Return in what way? Why?

2 Why, as you understand it, does the speaker say lines 30-32? What kind of 'solace' – comfort – (l 33) do you imagine the speaker would get?

3 Alliteration, you might know, is the repetition of a consonantal sound at the beginning of words that are near together. What is the sound used for alliteration in 'folded in the fist of the forest' (l 5)? Apart from being alliterative, what metaphor (comparison) does it insert into the poem? Are there any other metaphors in the poem?

4 Compare this poem with *Memories of a Grasscutter* (p31).

A Slave's Lament on Leaving Home p38

1 Which land is referred to as 'this land again' (l 2)? What do you suppose Aburi and Akwamu are?

2 Who do you imagine are 'these hard men' (l 9)? Why are they described as 'clear eye'd like the water we ride' (l 10)? Which happenings in the experience of a slave being brought from Africa are put into the poem? Why?

3 How do you interpret 'our blood mixed . . . ancestors' (ll 16-20)? Where would you say the 'chained and welcoming port' (l 26) might be? Why do you suppose the word 'new' is used as many as six times in four lines?

Father p39

1 Paddy is rice before it is husked. A kurtah (l 12) is a loose shirt or tunic that Hindus wear. Hillary (l 21) was a climber who reached the top of Mount Everest, the highest peak in the world. Sir Walter Raleigh (l 45) was a sixteenth century adventurer who found the Pitch Lake, in La Brea, Trinidad, on his way to look for Manoa, the fabled city of gold in South America. What work do you understand that the father did? What was 'a pitch-oil tin' (l 6) used for? What made 'hillocks' (l 17)? Where? How do you interpret lines 26-27? Which 'muffler' do you think 'snorted' (l 32)? What 'loads' (l 42) did animals wait for?

2 What meaning do you give to lines 22-24? 29-31? What picture or image do you see with 'A pitchyard thrust back/Our home' (ll 37-38)? Why is Hillary (l 21) referred to? Why Raleigh? How do you interpret lines 13-14? From what is said in lines 34-36, what do you think an 'aarti' is?

3 Which of these tones do you hear in the voice of the speaker:
a) discontentment b) disgust c) wishfulness d) amusement. Say why.

Sunday in the Lane p41

1 Which days of the week are told of in the poem? What is heard in the lane on Saturday? What is called 'a giant broom' (l 10)? Which examples of 'the week's worries' (l 11) are mentioned? Who has such worries?

2 Why do you suppose the speaker in the poem says 'church heavies the gentle air' (l 2)? What is called 'syrup' (l 5)? How does Sunday begin? Explain what you think line 20 is describing. How do you suppose 'the Lord comes down in radio glory' (l 22)?

3 What happens while the pious customs of Sunday are being followed? Who or what are referred to as 'Sunday brothers' (l 24)? Would you agree that the poem weaves together a marriage of contrasts? Say why, or why not. Do you find anything ironic in what is described? What part, would you say, do sounds play in producing the atmosphere of the poem?

Contre Jour p42

1 Who are the mothers referred to as 'those gentle scented mothers' (18)? What meaning would you give to 'It was never summer for her' (l 11)? Which lines tell the kind of house the mother of the speaker in the poem had?

2 How would you interpret lines 19-20? What do you understand by 'her life recedes' (l 21)? The mother 'once minced across the lawn' (l 22). Whose lawn? Why was she there? Whose photographs had 'frames of silver' (l 25)? Whose trays did she polish every week? Why? What was her reward?

3 'my mother would say' (l 13). What did she say? The French phrase 'contre jour' means against the daylight, but 'jour' also means day. Who said that phrase to the 'I' in the poem? When? Why did it start the 'I' thinking about what is in the poem?

Charity p43

1 Say what you take each of these to mean: 'trivializing everything' (l 2); 'down a peg' (6); 'knocked the stuffing out' (l 7); 'windfalls' (l 12). Point out how lines 1-8 make you think the speaker in the poem seems to be right that 'Trouble has done her good' (l 1). Would you say that in those lines the speaker seems pleased that the 'she' has benefited from having trouble in life?

2 'she looks more deserving' (l 9). Deserving of what? What is meant by 'to throw a rope to' (l 10)? To whom would you 'send your old blouses' (l 11)? What then is the speaker really pleased about? Do you ever feel pleased about being luckier or superior in some way to someone? What is the hypocrisy that lines 10-12 expose?

3 What is ironic or sarcastic about the title of the poem? In what way would you explain that the use of contrast gives the poem its very strong irony? What do you think was the purpose the poet had in mind in making this poem?

Flint p43

1 What do you take 'the retaliation of the sun' (l 2) to mean? What did it seem to cause?
2 When flint stones are struck together they spark. What happened with these 'colliding flint stones' (l 13)? And then 'when the land was still again' (l 16)?
3 What did the people think brought that calamity into their lives? What did they do? How did the wind come into the story?
4 Could this poem be an allegory (a story which, while telling one narrative, also signifies another story about the persons and events)? Ask yourself if some other calamity to the country could really be meant? If you think it might be an allegory, say what ther real story could be.

Hawk p44

1 How would you translate 'he will sell/his supremacy dear' (ll 5-6)? The 'uninitiated' (l 8) are those who do not yet know. What deceives the uninitiated' (l 8)? What 'spells threat, death' (l 11)?
2 'Director' (l 12) refers to the head of the United States agency for spying, the CIA; and 'Al Capone' (l 13) was a notorious gangster of the 1930s. Why do you suppose the hawk is compared to them?
3 'He does not intend to stay long up there' (l 19-20). What is he going to do?
4 What irony do you notice in how the hawk appears to the uninitiated and what he does as 'real hawk' (l 21)? Do you see the irony that is intended in the last line of the poem?

There was an Indian
J.C. Squire   *England*

There was an Indian, who had known no change,
    Who strayed content along a sunlit beach
Gathering shells. He heard a sudden strange
    Commingled[1] noise: looked up; and gasped for speech.

5 For in the bay, where nothing was before,
    Moved on the sea, by magic, huge canoes,
With bellying cloths on poles, and not one oar,
    And fluttering coloured signs and clambering crews.

And he, in fear, this naked man alone,
10   His fallen hands forgetting all their shells,
His lips gone pale, knelt low behind a stone,
    And stared, and saw, and did not understand,
Columbus's doom[2]-burdened caravels[3]
    Slant to the shore, and all their seamen land.

[1] *commingled* – mixed together
[2] *doom* – ruin and death
[3] *caravels* – sailing ships

Absence
Elizabeth Jennings   *England*

I visited the place where we last met.
Nothing was changed, the gardens were well-tended,
The fountains sprayed their usual steady jet;
There was no sign that anything had ended
5 And nothing to instruct me to forget.
The thoughtless birds that shook out of the trees,
Singing an ecstasy I could not share,
Played cunning in my thoughts. Surely in these
Pleasures there could not be a pain to bear
10 Or any discord shake the level breeze.

It was because the place was just the same
That made your absence seem a savage force,
For under all the gentleness there came
An earthquake tremor: fountain, birds and grass
15 Were shaken by my thinking of your name.

In the Attic
Andrew Motion *England*

Even though we know now
your clothes will never
be needed, we keep them,
upstairs in a locked trunk.

5 Sometimes I kneel there,
holding them, trying to relive
time you wore them, to remember
the actual shape of arm and wrist.

My hands push down between
10 hollow, invisible sleeves,
hesitate, then lift
patterns of memory:

a green holiday, a red christening,
all your unfinished lives
15 fading through dark summers,
entering my head as dust.

Beverly Is Dead
Susan Brown *Virgin Islands*

Beverly is dead.
She died away in New York
so they sent her home on Pan Am

and they iced her in the clinic
5   till the flowers came from Fla.
Then, in the morning, Sunday, women
gathered at Miss Hattie's
to fix the wreaths for Beverly.
They pinned Miss Mary's lilies in
10 with real red roses
and Joyce put Madagascar jasmine and
bloody bouganvilla to tie with oleander,
pink, Beverly's favourite color.
Mammoth leaves and new carnations wept
15 in a plastic pail on the padded mahogany table
while Miss Hattie's maid stepped lightly
with iced tea in Danish glasses.
And the cluttered pantry chocked itself
with fragrance and with ribbons
20 (the last wreath hung for safety
on the ice box door).
And all the while Miss Hattie snapping pictures
with her Kodak,
to keep alive the busy hands of death.

An Ageing Lady
Edward Baugh   *Jamaica*

You'd never think,
seeing her step so prim
and whalebone-straight to church,
dropping like scented handkerchiefs,
5   now here, now there, a smile –
you'd never think
so much calamity[1] licked at her heels.

Her God had blessed her womb;
six children were her harvest-gift.
10 Raised them to her image of prissy perfection,
testaments[2] of virtue for the tongue-wagging town.
The blight, when it revealed itself, was cruel.

Two long since are mad,
And one of those her only son.
15 Two others, fragile spinsters, whose
pale, proud hands have known
no toil or tenderness,
flutter on the edge of the abyss.
The other two – a tale of bitter marriages.

20 Watch her now
this Harvest-Sunday morning
sidle splendidly and late into her pew,
attended by her ghostly retinue[3]
of spinster daughters.
25 She turned to ask the number of the hymn,
then, aiming at the rafters a youthful vibrato,
out-worships her neighbours and magnifies her Lord.

On arch and altar-rail the offerings bloom.

[1] *calamity* – misfortune
[2] *testaments* – proofs, tributes, perfect examples
[3] *retinue* – followers

Uncle Time
Dennis Scott *Jamaica*

Uncle Time is a ole, ole man . . .
All year long 'im wash 'im foot in de sea,
long, lazy years on de wet san'
an' shake de coconut tree dem
5 quiet-like wid 'im sea-win' laughter,
scraping away de lan' . . .

Uncle Time is spider-man, cunnin' an' cool,
him tell yu: watch de hill an' yu se mi.
Huhn! Fe yu yi no quick enough fe si
10 how 'im move like mongoose; man, yu tink 'im fool?

Me Uncle Time smile black as sorrow;
'im voice is sof' as bamboo leaf
but Lawd, me Uncle cruel.
When 'im play in de street
15 wid yu woman – watch 'im! By tomorrow
she dry as cane-fire, bitter as cassava;
an' when 'im teach yu son, long after
yu walk wid stranger, an' yu bread is grief.
Watch how 'im spin web roun' yu house, an' creep
20 inside; an' when im' touch yu, weep . . .

Do not go Gentle into that Good Night
Dylan Thomas   *Wales*

Do not got gentle into that good night,
Old age should burn and rave at close of day;
Rage, rage against the dying of the light.

Though wise men at their end know dark is right,
5 Because their words have forked no lightning they
Do not go gentle into that good night.

Good men, the last wave by, crying how bright
Their frail deeds might have danced in a green bay,
Rage, rage against the dying of the light.

10 Wild men who caught and sang the sun in flight,
And learn, too late, they grieved it on its way,
Do not go gentle into that good night.

Grave men, near death, who see with blinding sight
Blind eyes could blaze like meteors and be gay,
15 Rage, rage against the dying of the light.

And you, my father, there on the sad height,
Curse, bless, me now with your fierce tears, I pray.
Do not go gentle into that good night.
Rage, rage against the dying of the light.

Lines to a Friend and Fellow Survivor Rediscovered After a Space of Twenty Years

Gloria Escoffery *Jamaica*

I am no longer what I was:
not 'longer in the tooth' but
possessing fewer molars today
I have a sharper tooth for reality.

5 You, I daresay, are no longer
what I had vaguely thought you must be.
Like me, you must have learnt by now
you never were whatever you thought you were.

Till next week, or tomorrow,
10 or for the count of ten if you prefer,
I am what I think I have always been: strong.
You must know, as I do, that pits have sides to
     climb out by.

My fingers are crooked,
my hand clasp weaker than it was,
15 the paint brush seems to go its own way
and I allow it the miracle of making its own mark.
My back is cranky and the vertebrae rap together;
they have no quarrel with the board beneath the mattress.
Knees and ankles complain in their own way
20 while feet exercise the rights of their lease with
     less of the old spring.

Too Soon it was My Allotted Task

Edward Anthony Watson *Barbados*

Too soon was it was my allotted task
to drag my father's past
from drawers and closets
to see him clothed again
5 in colours more splendid
than funeral blackness.

This was not the time
to bewilder myself with memories
but to pass on to others
10 the providence of a simple life:

the bright suits and shirts;
shoes; dozens of neck-ties,
every colour from red to green
faded into an ashen grey;
15 stiff collars in a collar-box;
hats, a cummerbund, a cane:

these and more, would go
to the Veterans of Foreign Wars.
There were other things,
20 mementos that I have kept:
a pharmaceutical note-book
containing five formulae
and a slip of paper
with a detailed budget
25 marked simply, "July, 1938,"
the economy of yesterday in a proud hand,
the present dead, riding forever
on a moment's wing;
two pairs of cuff-links,
30 and a small pocket-knife.

In the end, these will take on
their own magnificence,
perhaps when my son
will no longer wear his sleeves unbuttoned
35 now that there are silver links
to chain him to my past.

¹ *cummerbund* – waistband

Lights Out
Edward Thomas   *England*

I have come to the borders of sleep,
The unfathomable deep
Forest where all must lose
Their way, however straight,
5 Or winding, soon or late;
They cannot choose.

Many a road and track
That, since the dawn's first crack,
Up to the forest brink,
10 Deceived the travellers,
Suddenly now blurs,
And in they sink.

Here love ends,
Despair, ambition ends;
15 All pleasure and all trouble,
Although most sweet or bitter,
Here ends in sleep that is sweeter
Than tasks most noble.

There is not any book
20 Or face of dearest look
That I would not turn from now
To go into the unknown
I must enter, and leave, alone,

I know not how.
25 The tall forest towers;
Its cloudy foliage lowers
Ahead, shelf above shelf;
Its silence I hear and obey
That I may lose my way
30 And myself.

Bookmark
Raymond Barrow *Belize*

Deep in the heart, beyond all sight, there lies
A volume of those long-remembered things
Which, in the gloom of sorrows and of sighs
Crept forth and sang of hope a stout faith brings.
5 And from these things has drawn, this heart of mine,
Comfort and succour that will prove full meed[1]
When in the drought of ageing years I pine
For sustenance in some small hour of need.

Clear on each page they are; a touch of hand
10 In sympathy; or laughter of surprise;
Or morn of beauty; or some romping band
Of children with adventure in their eyes.

And yet invisibly, a knife-like blade
Marks where one beam brought sunlight to my shade.

[1] *meed* – reward

Elegy
Anthony McNeill *Jamaica*

She tripped over a stone on a bright evening.
Rose tints in the air
And the sun dancing.

Carried bleeding off to the hospital,
5 The doctors tinkered with her for three days,
Then death came on a white horse and took her away.

And where she is now I just couldn't say,
Being only a foolish father,
But minds like telescopes promise a place

10 Of instant wisdom, where answers are given at once;
Not suited, I think, for my little angel who skipped and ran,
Her questions cartwheeling all day in the sun.

Discussion and Activities

There Was an Indian p52

1 What Indian is meant? What does he see as 'huge canoes' (l 6) and 'bellying clothes on poles (l 7)? Why does he notice 'not one oar' (l 7) and think of magic? What effect did the sight have on him?

2 From what the poem contains, what was the life of the Indian like before the caravels came?

3 Why do you think that the poet described the caravels as 'doom-burdened' (l 13)? What does this word tell you about the poet's feeling and attitude? Would you say the poem was written more to give a descriptive account of the landing of Columbus or more to express a sorrow about the Arawaks and Caribs? What guides you in your judgement?

4 What do the *sounds* of these words suggest to your ear? – commingled (l 4); b) fluttering (l 8); clambering (l 8).

Absence p52

1 Why would someone say that this poem is a love poem? Why, do you imagine, does the speaker ask something 'to instruct me to forget' (l 5)? Forget what or whom? What would you say 'Played cunning in my thoughts' (l 8) means? How did the birds seem to feel as they sang? Was that how the speaker also felt? What were the 'Pleasures' referred to in line 9?

2 Why do you suppose the speaker spoke of 'a pain to bear' (l 9)? What pain is being experienced? What contrast is put in in lines 11-12? How, according to the poem, did an earthquake tremor occur? How do the phrases 'Nothing was changed' (l 2), 'no sign that anything had ended' (l 4), and 'the place was just the same' (l 11) stress the frame of mind of the 'I' in the poem?

3 Do you detect any kind of romantic exaggeration or 'poetic' posture in the poem at all? Pay attention to the metaphors used and consider how natural or forced each one is. Does the use of rhythm, in your opinion, help or hinder the kind of mood the poet wants the poem to have? Work out the rhyme scheme for each stanza and ask yourself whether the rhymes flowed easily into the poem or whether the poet forced in phrases and words to keep rhyming.

In the Attic p53

1 An attic is a small room up under the roof of a house, a garret. What is kept 'in a locked trunk' (l 4)? Why will they 'never/be needed' (ll 2-3)?

2 How is the speaker in the poem 'Trying to relive' (l 6) something? What? Why do you think the speaker tries to do that? How do you interpret line 12? What does line 13 tell you?

3 With what tone of voice do you hear the last three lines being said by the speaker? How do those lines wrap up the whole poem in them?

4 Compare this poem with *Too Soon it was My Allotted Task* (p58) looking for similarities and differences.

Beverly is Dead p53

1 'Fla' (l 5) is short for Florida. What is coming from Florida? For what reason? Why is Pan Am – the airline – mentioned? What do you understand by 'iced her in the clinic' (l 4)?

2 Which flowers were arranged? Why did the maid have 'iced tea' (l 17)? As what figure of speech is the word 'wept' (l 14) used? Where else is such a comparison made?

3 *Personification* is speaking of animals or things or ideas as if they were human beings with human abilities and qualities. Where is personification used in the poem?

4 The last three lines of the poem turn your attention to Miss Hattie and what she did. Would you say that the poem is not about Beverly but about how her friends enjoyed the occasion? Say why or why not. Does it seem to have any *satire* in it – a humorous way of ridiculing silly things people think or do?

An Ageing Lady p54

1 In the simile 'dropping like scented handkerchiefs' (l 4), what were dropped? How do you interpret the metaphor 'calamity licked at her heels' (l 7)? Who 'are mad' (l 13)? A spinster is an unmarried woman. Who are 'fragile spinsters' (l 15)? Why 'fragile'? What 'abyss' (l 18) – deep or bottomless pit – are they on the edge of?

2 Where is the ageing lady 'this Harvest-Sunday morning' (l 21)? How would you interpret lines 23-24? At harvest time, as you know, people reap the rewards of their labour. What is the irony to be

noticed between the fact that it is Harvest-Sunday and the facts of the events of her life? What do you suppose is 'a youthful vibrato' she aims 'at the rafters' (l 26)? Which 'offerings' bloom (l 28)? How does that deepen the irony of the situation?

Uncle Time p55

1 As you see, this poem is in the Jamaican dialect of English. Is it in dialect to amuse the readers? Does it deal with something amusing? Give your reason for what you think.
2 Which lines tell you that time seems to stay in one place for a long while? Which lines then tell you that time moves so slyly that before they know it time makes cruel changes in people?
3 Calling time *Uncle Time* is *personification*, a kind of metaphor or comparison in which an animal, thing, or idea is spoken of as if it has human qualities. Point out all the places in the poem where you detect something said metaphorically.

Do not go Gentle into that Good Night p56

1 Who is asking whom not to 'go gentle into that good night'? What 'good night' is meant? What is the person being asked to do instead? What other men does the poet say 'do not go gentle'?
2 Can you explain what the poet has said of each of these? – wise men; good men; wild men; grave men.

Lines Written to a Friend and Fellow Survivor p57

1 'longer in the tooth' (l 2) means with the gums showing more of the teeth, a slightly humorous way of saying 'older'. 'molars' (l 3) are teeth. How would you interpret line 4?
2 'learnt by now/you never were whatever you thought you were' (l 8). Is that said about the friend, about the 'I', or about everybody at a certain age? Why does the 'I' say 'Till next week, or tomorrow,/or for the count of ten' (ll 9-10)?
3 What 'pits' (l 12) do you think are meant? Why do you suppose the 'I' mentions 'the paint brush' (l 16)? How do you interpret 'the miracle of making its own mark' (l 17)?
4 How does the last stanza (lines 17-21) bear out the claim 'I have a sharper tooth for reality' (l 4)? What then would you say is the tone (the feeling or attitude in the voice) of the poem? a) anger and bitterness; b) sadness about oneself; c) acceptance of change.

Too Soon it was My Allotted Task p58

1 'to drag my father's past' (l 2). What was the allotted task? Why "too soon'? 'to pass on to others' (l 9). Pass on what? To which others? Which items are called 'the providence of a simple life' (l 10)?

2 In what sense is the phrase 'to see him do that again' (l 4) used? Why do you think the 'I' said lines 7-8?

3 A budget is a statement of how money is going to be spent. Why do you suppose the speaker used the word 'economy' (l 26)? Which articles did he/she keep as mementos?

4 Do you know what cuff-links are? The word 'links' (l 35) is used with two meanings. What are they? How would you translate 'to chain him to my past' (l 36) What is implied in 'no longer wears his sleeves unbuttoned' (l 34)?

5 Compare this poem with *In The Attic*, looking for any similarities and differences.

Lights Out p59

1 'Lights out' is the time when persons in institutions like boarding schools, orphanages and the army have to be in bed and turn all lights off. It is the end of the activities of the day. Do you think this poem is about that time or about some other time? Do you think the 'sleep' (l 1) is what you do every night or some other kind of sleep? What do you make of 'where all must lose their way' (l 3-4)?

2 'Here love ends' (ll 13). What else ends? Does the 'I' welcome the end to such things? Why, do you imagine, does the 'I' say it is 'sleep that is sweeter/Than tasks most noble' (ll 17-18)? How would you interpret 'the unknown/
I must enter, and leave alone,/I know not how' (ll 22-24)?

3 The 'I' speaks of 'Forest' (l 3), 'their way' (l 4), 'road and track' (l 7). Are these to be taken literally or are they figures of speech making comparisons by saying one thing is something else (metaphors)? Give reasons for your interpretations.

Bookmark p60

1 As with all poems, read this one aloud a few times before discussing it. 'Full meed' (l 6) means full reward or repayment. From what does the 'I' say 'this heart of mine' (l 5) 'has drawn' (l 5) 'comfort and succour' (l 6)?

2 What is the volume (l 2), or book, a book of? When do they bring 'a stout faith' (l 4)? When the 'I' says 'Clear on each page' (l 9) is he talking of the page of a book or of something else? If something else, what? What things are on that page?
3 Which line tells you that with all the other things there is something especially remembered? Why is it special?
4 Although the language of the poem is out-of-date, perhaps old-fashioned, would you say the feeling it presents is false and hypocritical, or a genuine feeling the 'I' felt? How would you describe the feeling the 'I' means to communicate to a reader? Why?

Elegy p60

1 What events are related in the first two stanzas? What contrasts with the occurrence of the tripping? Does this contrast increase or lessen how the poem makes you feel?
2 What tone of voice do you hear where the poet uses 'tinkered' (l 5); 'only a foolish father' (l 8); 'promise' (l 9)?
3 What lines are most heavily sarcastic and bitter? Which lines are saddest?
4 Are sad poems not enjoyable because they are sad?

5 Creativity and Endeavour

The Lonely Farmer
R.S. Thomas   Wales

Poor hill farmer astray in the grass:
There came a movement and he looked up, but
All that he saw was the wind pass.
There was a sound of voices on the air,
5   But where, where? It was only the glib stream talking
Softly to itself. And once when he was walking
Along a lane in spring he was deceived
By a shrill whistle coming through the leaves:
Wait a minute, wait a minute – four swift notes;
10 He turned, and it was nothing, only a thrush
In the thorn bushes easing its throat.
He swore at himself for paying heed,
The poor hill farmer, so often again
Stopping, staring, listening, in vain,
15 His ear betrayed by the heart's need.

Trane
Edward Brathwaite   Barbados

Propped against the crowded bar
he pours into the curved and silver horn
his old unhappy longing for a home
the dancers twist and turn
5   he leans and wishes he could burn
his memories to ashes like some old notorious emperor

of rome. But no stars blazed across the sky when he was born
no wise men found his hovel; this crowded bar
where dancers twist and turn,
10 holds all the fame and recognition he will ever earn
on earth or heaven. He leans against the bar
and pours his old unhappy longing in the saxophone.

Cynddylan on a Tractor
R.S. Thomas   *Wales*

Ah, you should see Cynddylan on a tractor.
Gone the old look that yoked him to the soil;
He's a new man now, part of the machine,
His nerves of metal and his blood oil.
5 The clutch curses, but the gears obey
His least bidding, and lo, he's away
Out of the farmyard, scattering hens.
Riding to work now as a great man should,
He is the knight at arms breaking the fields'
10 Mirror of silence, emptying the wood
Of foxes and squirrels and bright jays.
The sun comes over the tall trees
Kindling all the hedges, but not for him
Who runs his engine on a different fuel.
15 And all the birds are singing, bills wide in vain,
As Cynddylan passes proudly up the lane.

Dives
Edward Brathwaite   *Barbados*

Before they built the deep water harbour
sinking an island to do it
we used to row out in our boats

to the white liners, great ocean-going floats,
5 to dive for coins. Womens with bracelets,
men with expensive tickers on their wrists,

watched us through bland sun glasses
so that their blue stares never blinked.
they tossed us pennies, the spinning flat
10 metallic bird would hit the water with a little

flap and wing zig-zagging down the water's track.
Our underwater eyes would watch it like a cat
as it dark bottomed soundwards like a pendulum
winging from side to side, now black

15 now bright, now black, now bright,
catching the dying daylight down
the coal dark sides of the ship
every shadow we saw was a possible shark

but we followed that flat dark light
20 even if the propellers would suddenly turn
burning the water to murderous cold
we would never come nearer to gold.

The Washerwomen
Owen Campbell   *St Vincent*

Down where the river beats itself against the stones
And washes them in clouds of frothy spray,
Or foaming, fumbles through them with the thousand tones
Of an orchestra,
5 The women wash, and humming keep a sort of time;
And families of bubbles frisk and float away
To be destroyed,
Like all the baffled hopes that had their little suns,
Tossed on the furious drifts of disappointments.
10 But all the tide
Cradles these clinging bubbles ever still, alike
The friendly little hopes that never leave the heart.
In this big hall of rushing waters women wash
And with the sound of washing,
15 With the steady heaving of their slender shoulders

As they rub their stubborn rags upon the boulders,
They keep a sort of time . . .

With their thoughts. These were unchanging
Like the persistent[1] music here,
20 Of swirling waters,
The crash of wet clothes beaten on the stones,
The sound of wind in leaves,
Or frog croaks after dusk, and the low moan
Of the big sea fighting the river's mouth.

25 The ever changing patterns in the clouds
Before their dissolution into rain;
Or the gay butterflies manoeuvring
Among the leafy camouflage[2] that clothes the banks
And hides their spent remains when they collapse and die,
30 Are symbols of their hopes and gaudy[3] plans
Which once they dreamt. But finally they learn to hope
And make plans less elaborate.
It was the same
With those that washed before them here
35 And passed leaving the soap-stained stones
Where others now half stoop like devotees
To pagan gods.

They have resigned themselves to daylong swishing
Of wet cloth chafing the very stone;
40 And the big symphony of waters rushing
Past clumps of tall stems standing alone,
Apart, like band-leaders, or sentinels,
They must hear the heavy hum
Of wings of insects overgrown,
45 Cleaving the air like bombers on a plotted course.
They must hear the long "hush" of the wind in leaves
As dead ones flutter down like living things
Until the shadows come.

[1] *persistent* – continuing
[2] *camouflage* – disguise
[3] *gaudy* – overdone, bright

For the 4th Grade, Prospect School: How I Became a Poet

J.A. Emanuel   *USA*

My kite broke loose,
took all my string
and backed into the sun.
I followed far as I could go
5 and high as I could run.

My special top went spinning
down the gutter, down the drain.
I heard it gurgling sideways,
saw it grinning in the rain,
10 my string wrapped around it
while I reached for it in vain.

My dog got thin and went away.
He took his leash – the wrapping string
that we pretended was a rope –
15 and went as far as he could hope
to find the sickbed where I lay.

And now, when I remember strings
and how they bind together things,
and how they stretch (like reach and run),
20 and hold (like hope) and give (like sun),
I tie together things I know
and wind up with a poem to show.

Carnival Sunday Jump-Up
Cecil Gray   *Trinidad and Tobago*

Carnival will spill out tomorrow and run
over the streets. But today we keep it
contained in backyards like this one,
with music more drunkening than rum.
5 We jump-up, happy and helpless. We were
christened to keep faith with the beat
of calypsoes and the sanctus of drums.

The crowd thickens and rolls like an ocean
washing its billows across the whole lawn.
10 This one is up on a hill and below us
the Gulf, in costume already, all satins and
sequins, is dancing as if Jour Ouvert[1] has come.
Hill or no hill, we jump-up and jump-up.
I shuffle and move to the side to sit down.

15 Two English critics, accents heavy with pounds
of patronage they can't spend in England,
and finding the strong rhythm too difficult,
waylay me to talk, raising their voices to
stickfight[2] with the jamming[3] about language
20 most appropriate to West Indian verse.
I take it they're playing Pierrot Grenade.[4]

But I listen as well as I can since
it is Carnival. It has to be patois, like
calypsoes, they say; and anything metrical
25 is aping what's foreign. (Hanging one's
hat, etc.) I think. The feet tramp the grass
keeping time with a metre even the new
colonisers can hear. They continue.

Since our experience is black, and
30 somewhat incestuous, we must stick to
a language of anger born in grim ghettoes
of squalor where history shuts out laughter

and dance. Those who had essayed (their word)
outside natural limits had failed, falling
35 somewhere between Shakespeare and Larkin.

Verse raises its volume in the loudspeakers
and I slip slyly away to dance the vernacular.
It is Carnival and each one, local or not,
is allowed to spout robber talk[5] without limit.
40 So I don't say to them I want to jump-up
in time down the hill although I might fall
somewhere between Walcott and Naipaul.

[1] *Jour Ouvert* – the first hours of Carnival in Trinidad
[2] *stickfight* – a fighting game with sticks
[3] *jamming* – dancing in a crowd together
[4] *Pierrot Grenade* – a Trinidad masquerader who pretends to be a professor and gives instruction about the English language
[5] *robber talk* – exaggerated language used by Trinidad masqueraders called 'robbers'

Letter to England
Bruce St John   *Barbados*

Girl chile darling yuh ole muddah hay
Praisin' de Lord fuh 'E blessing an' 'E mercies
You is many many blessin's an' all o' me mercies
Glory to God!
5 Uh get de 5 pound an' de Christmas card
God bless yuh!
But de carpenter ain' come to put on de shed-roof
So uh spen' it an uh sen' Rosy pretty to de
Exhibition gal, yuh should see she!
10 Next month when yuh sen me allowance again,
We will see wuh kin happen in de name o' de Lord.
De Cashmere sweater dat yuh sen' muh so soft
An so warm, uh kin nevah fuget muh
Poor li'l' chile. Sister Reed can'
15 Brag pun me like before, tink she one got
Daughter in England? Uh wear um down to

Service t'ree Sunday mornin' straight an'
Den all bout de place fuh to show dem
I en common, but Lord I haffa tell yuh
20 Dat it ketch 'pon a nail in de kitchen, so,
Bless you love don' f'get to sen' anedduh one,
Uh paint up de place an' varnish de furnitures
An' Lord mek peace dat t'ief charge muh so
High dat I ain't got a cent lef' to brighten
25 Muh face, so de Lord will bless yuh
Don' fo'get you ole muddah, lonely
An' t'ankful, wukkin' she finger to de
Bone, she soul case droppin' out, Wuh law!
I does pray day an' night fuh yuh
30 Come back child, I does cry, I does grieve but

De Lord unde'stand, I closes now
Wid love an' gratitude, care yuhself
Doan le' da man dat yuh married
To upset yuh, le' de Lord
35 An' yuh poor ole muddah keep a
Place in yuh heart. Amen. Amen.

A Sea Chantey
Derek Walcott   *St Lucia*

La, tout n'est qu'ordre et beauté,
Luxe calme, et volupté.
Anguilla, Adina,
Antigua, Cannelles,
5 Andreuille, all the L's
Voyelles, of the liquid Antilles,
The names tremble like needles
Of anchored frigates,
Yachts tranquil as lilies,
10 In ports of calm coral,
The lithe,[1] ebony hulls
Of strait-stitching schooners,

The needles of their masts
That thread archipelagoes
15 Refracted[2] embroidery
In feverish waters
Of the sea-farer's islands,
Their shorn, leaning palms,
Shaft of Odysseus,
20 Cyclopic volcanoes,
Creak their own histories,
In the peace of green anchorage;

Flight, and Phyllis,
Returned from Grenadines,
25 Names entered this sabbath,
In the port-clerk's register;
Their baptismal names,
The sea's liquid letters,
Repos donnez à cils . . .
30 And their blazing cargoes
Of charcoal and oranges;
Quiet, the fury of their ropes.
Daybreak is breaking
On the green chrome water,
35 The white herons of yachts
Are at sabbath communion,
The histories of schooners
Are murmured in coral,
Their cargoes of sponges
40 On sandpits of islets
Barques white as white salt
Of acrid Saint Maarten,
Hulls crusted with barnacles,[3]
Holds foul with great turtles,
45 Whose ship-boys have seen
The blue heave of Leviathan,
A sea-faring, Christian,
And intrepid people.
Now an apprentice[4] washes his cheeks
50 With salt water and sunlight.

In the middle of the harbour
A fish breaks the Sabbath
With a silvery leap.
The scales fall from him
55 In a tinkle of church bells;
The town streets are orange
With the week-ripened sunlight,
Balanced on the bowsprit,[5]
A young sailor is playing
60 His grandfather's chantey
On a trembling mouth-organ.

The music curls, dwindling
Like smoke from blue galleys,
To dissolve near the mountains.
65 The music uncurls with
The soft vowels of inlets,
The christening of vessels,
The titles of portages,
The colours of sea-grapes,
70 The tartness of sea-almonds,
The alphabet of church-bells,
The peace of white horses,
The pastures of ports,
The litany of islands,
75 The rosary of archipelagoes,
Anguilla, Antigua,
Virgin of Guadeloupe,
And stone-white Grenada
Of sunlight and pigeons
80 The amen of calm waters,
The amen of calm waters,
The amen of calm waters.

[1] *lithe* – flexible, moving easily
[2] *refracted* – reflected, crookedly
[3] *barnacles* – shells that stick on
[4] *apprentice* – learner
[5] *bowsprit* – a bar or pole from a ship's nose or prow

Nomads

Barnabas J. Ramon-Fortuné   *Trinidad and Tobago*

The nomads[1] of the sea have creased their tents
And lie at anchor rocking in the bay;
A-doze in the warm sun of indolence.[2]
They reminisce[3] of how, through tossing spray,
5   They forced their furrows from far continents,
Shot skirting by the shores of Uruguay
Their keels astrain and all their canvas bent
To catch the urging clamour of the wind;
And how, amid the busy noise of harbours,
10 They loaded many tons of golden-skinned
Bananas from Jamaica, fruit from the arbours
Of the Leeward Isles, and through the finned,
Blue waters of Barbados speeded on
Through ocean lakes, their rigging spread upon
15 The speckless blue, their prows toward the sun;
And how, in some Pacific Port, they lay
Panting from their wild journey through the foam
Among the sampans in the littered bay!

(How far is home! How far – how far is home!)

20 Till setting sail again, and grinding back
Their anchors, spreading their canvas free,
And nosing between tug and yacht and smack,
They brave the wild adventure of the sea!
But now they lie a-doze upon the bay,
25 These nomads of the sea, spent journey-weary,
Rubbing their shoulders on the littered quay.
Rest is the end of toil: but there's no rest
For these dark, sun-burned wanderers of the sea
Forever roaming over the briny prairie,
30 Only a little breathing space, at best.

[1] *nomads* – wanderers
[2] *indolence* – laziness
[3] *reminisce* – think about the past

Milking Before Dawn
Ruth Dallas   *New Zealand*

In the drifting rain the cows in the yard are as black
And wet and shiny as rocks in an ebbing tide;
But they smell of the soil, as leaves lying under trees
Smell of the soil, damp and steaming, warm.
5 The shed is an island of light and warmth, the night
Was water-cold and starless out in the paddock.

Crouched on the stool, hearing only the beat
The monotonous beat and hiss of the smooth machines,
The choking gasp of the cups and rattle of hooves,
10 How easy to fall asleep again, to think
Of the man in the city asleep; he does not feel
The night encircle him, the grasp of mind.

But now the hills in the east return, are soft
And grey with mist, the night recedes, and the rain.
15 The earth as it turns towards the sun is young
Again, renewed, its history wiped away
Like the tears of a child. Can the earth be young again
And not the heart? Let the man in the city sleep.

Discussion and Activities

The Lonely Farmer p67

1 How did 'the glib stream' (l 5) deceive the farmer? Where did he think 'a shrill whistle' (l 8) came from? Why do you think 'He swore at himself for paying heed' (l 12)? How would you interpret 'betrayed by the heart's need' (l 15)?

2 How does the speaker in the poem want you to feel about the farmer? How do you know? *Sentimentality* is an excess of emotion or feeling attached to a subject that does not merit a great amount of emotion. Do you find this poem sentimental? Is the farmer's situation and desire being exaggerated, or are there many people in a similar situation?

Trane p67

1 John Coltrane was an American jazz musician of outstanding talent. His friends described him as gentle and shy. What line of the poem tells you the instrument he played most? Why do you think the poet said Trane wished 'he could burn his memories to ashes' (ll 5 and 6). What other phrases and sentences tell you about his life?

2 What do you take lines 1 and 2 to mean? What feeling do you get, if any, from the poem? What things make you feel that way?

Cynddylan on a Tractor p68

1 Cynddylan (pronounced *Cun-thullan*) did not have a tractor before. True or false? What line or lines tell you?

2 What feeling does he now have? In which particular lines does the poet tell you this?

3 Could Cynddylan be a man of this country?

Dives p68

1 In Barbados there was a tiny islet where the deep water harbour now is, as said in line 2. Who tossed pennies? From where? Why? Why were they not thrown into the boats? What does 'blue' (l 8) tell you?

2 What is the poem doing in lines 9-17? Say which words or phrases there you find very useful in helping you to see and hear what is being communicated.
3 What does 'we would never come nearer to gold' (l 22) tell you about the ones who dived? How does that explain what is said in line 20?

The Washerwomen p69

1 What goes on in the women's minds while they wash? (Consider lines 8-13; 17-18; 30-32.)
2 The poet refers to music more than once. What things does he say make music? Is there anything else about the poem that goes with the idea of music? If so, illustrate what you mean.
3 Which of the images brought to your mind have any special feelings about them? Tell what the feeling is and whether it helps you enjoy the poem or not.
4 What tone of voice do you hear in lines 33-34? Where else do you hear the same tone? Does it have any importance in the poem?

For the 4th Grade, Prospect School: How I Became a Poet p71

1 Notice that in stanzas 1,2 and 3 the speaker in the poem tells of little misfortunes that happened to him. Do you think 'string' (l 2), (l 10), (l 13) is a symbol? Say why or why not.
2 Which line in the poem tells something a poet does? How would you interpret 'tie together' (l 21)? Would you agree that the strings in line 17 are words a poet uses to compose a poem, or not? Say why.

Carnival Sunday Jump-Up p72

1 Where is the Carnival Jump-up taking place? Why did the 'I' in the poem listen to what the critics had to say? What did he or she do when he or she had heard enough?
2 What did they mean by 'aping what's foreign' (l 25)? 'Hanging one's hat higher than one can reach' means trying to do what is beyond your ability. Which topics or themes did the critics say West Indians should stick to when they write? Why? Shakespeare and Larkin were English poets. Walcott and Naipaul are West Indian writers the world respects and admires. Neither of them does what the English

critics in the poem require. Why do you suppose the 'I' did not mind falling 'somewhere between Walcott and Naipaul' (l 42)?

3 The critics thought West Indians should avoid 'anything metrical' (l 24). Do you detect anything ironic or sarcastic in 'finding the strong rhythm too difficult' (l 17), 'The feet tramp the grass keeping time with a metre' (l 26), and 'to dance the vernacular' (l 37)? What was the music that was so metrical? Would you say that the 'I' agrees with the critics, or not? Who are called 'the new colonisers' (ll 27-8)? Why? What do you see as the attitude of the writer of this poem to such critics?

Letter to England p73

1 This poem is in the Barbadian dialect of English. Who sent 'de 5 pound note'? To whom? What was it for? What was it spent on?

2 A 'Cashmere sweater' (l 12) is too warm for places like Barbados. How was it important to the writer of the letter? What use was made of it? Why did the 'I' in the letter want 'aneddah one' (l 21)? 'I ain't got a cent lef' (l 24). What was the money spent on doing? How would you think of someone who said she was 'wukking she finger to de/Bone' (l 27) spending money that way?

3 What was it Sister Reed used to boast about? How could the sweater 'show them/I en common' (ll 18-19)? How did they seem to regard England and things from England?

4 What impression do you get of the person? Quote evidence from the poem. Do you think the poem has *satire* in it?

A Sea Chantey p74

1 This poem was written about forty years ago by Derek Walcott who was awarded the Nobel Prize for Literature – the world's greatest honour for a writer – in 1992. Even more than other poems it needs to be read aloud over and over.
   The Grenadines, as you might know, are islets between St Vincent and Grenada. A chantey is a sailor's song. How does the title fit the poem? How is 'litany' connected with a day of the week of the poem? What in line 75 has a similar connection? In what ways is the whole poem suggestive of a litany?

2 Besides Caribbean islands, what things are named in the poem (e.g. 'Flight', 'Phyllis')? What do they do? Where are they now? What is the 'green anchorage' (l 22)?

3 What are the comparisons made by the use of these words?
'needles' (ll 7 and 13); 'thread' (l 14); 'embroidery' (l 15); 'palms'
(l 18); 'washes' (l 49); 'horses' (l 72); 'litany' (l 74); 'rosary' (l 75)?
Which of these comparisons seem to suggest deeper comparisons?
What comparison is being made in lines 19-22?

4 Why, in your opinion, did the poet choose to end the poem with
those last three lines? Which of these feelings was the poem born
of: a) restlessness and excitement; b) disgust and scorn; c) love for a
place; d) laziness and boredom? Justify your opinion.

Nomads p77

1 Nomads are wanderers. Some live in tents. How soon do you know
who or what the nomads are in this poem?

2 'They reminisce' (l 4). What does that mean? Say in two words what
they are reminiscing about. Where are they now?

3 What do these lines mean: 1; 6; 17; 26; 29?

4 What is there in the poem that causes a sensation of pushing and
effort? Why is it there?

Milking Before Dawn p78

1 How do you know the milking is not being done by hand, but by
the modern method? Where is it being done? What was the night
like?

2 How many descriptive comparisons can you find in the first stanza?
In the second? The third? In what way do they play a part in this
particular poem?

3 In which lines does the poet say that with dawn the earth is young
again? What question does she then ask? Whose heart is she
referring to? Why?

4 Why does she say "Let the man in the city sleep"?

LEVEL 2

1 Love and Friendship

When Folks Like You Have Birthdays
Heather Royes *Jamaica*

When folks you like have birthdays,
the country should fire a 21-gun salute,
shout hip-hip-hurrah,
and blow all the ships' whistles in Kingston Harbour.

5   Instead, we had a curfew[1] – a sign of changing times.
Yet, it was most appropriate
that on your birthday we should feel
the changing times,
the crackle and crumble
10 of the old, hard crust
as the new breaks through.

So, on your birthday,
which was a nice enough May morning wrapped in blue,
we were unable to bring on the 21-gun salute
15 (though guns were firing),
shout hip-hip-hurrah (though shouting was heard),
or blow all the ships' whistles (though whistles were blown).

But as the curfew ended,
and the tanks crunched their way home,
20 the soldiers and policemen wearily shouldered their rifles,
and Kingston was back to normal . . .
we thought of you.

[1] *curfew* – rule that people must stay indoors after a certain time.

For My Mother
(May I Inherit Half Her Strength)
Lorna Goodison   *Jamaica*

my mother loved my father
I write this as an absolute[1]
in this my thirtieth year
the year to discard absolutes

5 he appeared, her fate disguised,
as a sunday player in a cricket match,
he had ridden from a country
one hundred miles south of hers.

She tells me he dressed the part,
10 visiting dandy, maroon blazer
cream serge pants, seam like razor,
and the beret and the two-tone shoes.

My father stopped to speak to her sister,
till he looked and saw her by the oleander,
15 sure in the kingdom of my blue-eyed grandmother.
He never played the cricket match that day.

He wooed her with words and he won her.
He had nothing but words to woo her,
On a visit to distant Kingston he wrote,

20 'I stood on the corner of King Street and looked,
and not one woman in that town was lovely as you'.

My mother was a child of the petit bourgeoisie[2]
studying to be a teacher, she oiled her hands
to hold pens.
25 My father barely knew his father, his mother died young,
he was a boy who grew with his granny.

My mother's trousseau[3] came by steamer through the snows of
    Montreal
where her sister Albertha of the cheekbones and the
perennial Rose, combed Jewlit backstreets with French-
30 turned names for Doris' wedding things.

Such a wedding Harvey River, Hanover, had never seen
Who anywhere had seen a veil fifteen chantilly yards long?
and a crepe de chine dress with inlets of silk godettes
and a neck-line clasped with jewelled pins!
35 And on her wedding day she wept. For it was a brazen bride in those
    days
who smiled.
and her bouquet looked for the world like a sheaf of wheat
against the unknown of her belly,
a sheaf of wheat backed by maidenhair fern, representing Harvey
    River
40 her face washed by something other than river water.

My father made one assertive[4] move, he took the
    imported cherub down
from the height of the cake and dropped it in the soft territory
between her breasts . . . and she cried.

When I came to know my mother many years later,
    I knew her as the figure
45 who sat at the first thing I learned to read: 'SINGER',
    and she breast-fed
my brother while she sewed; and she taught us to read
    while she sewed and
she sat in judgement over all our disputes as she sewed.

She could work miracles, she would make a garment
    from a square of cloth
in a span that defied time. Or feed twenty people on a
    stew made from
50 fallen-from-the-head cabbage leaves and a carrot and a
    cho-cho and a palmful
of meat.

And she rose early and sent us clean into the world
    and she went to bed in
the dark, for my father came in always last.

There is a place somewhere where my mother never
    took the younger ones
55 a country where my father with the always smile
my father whom all women loved, who had the
    perpetual quality of wonder
given only to a child . . . hurt his bride.
Even at his death there was this 'Friend' who stood
    by her side,
but my mother is adamant[5] that that has no place in
    the memory of
60 my father.

When he died, she sewed dark dresses for the women
    among us
and she summoned that walk, straight-backed, that she
    gave to us
and buried him dry-eyed.
Just that morning, weeks after
65 she stood delivering bananas from their skin
singing in that flat hill country voice
she fell down a note to the realization that she did
not have to be brave, just this once
and she cried.

70 For her hands grown coarse with raising nine children
for her body for twenty years permanently fat
for the time she pawned her machine for my sister's
Senior Cambridge fees
and for the pain she bore with the eyes of a queen

75 and she cried also because she loved him.

[1] *absolute* – unquestionable statement
[2] *petit bourgeoisie* – lower middle class
[3] *trousseau* – a bride's dresses, etc.
[4] *assertive* – positive, confident
[5] *adamant* – unyielding, inflexible

Pa

Victor Questel   *Trinidad and Tobago*

In the quiet of the dining-room
an ageing man sits huddled over scrambled eggs;
a copy of the *Guardian* drooling from his hands.
And in the silent rage of his broken posture,
5 he concludes how seldom he laughed in those years when he had
sharp two-toned shoes, double-breasted suits and
       steady hands.
Blanks circle him;
and yet those days when he rolled and pitched
the seas with the best, are a memory away.

10 He muses how committed he was to the corner stones
of his world. Rocks that once supported a fixed drive.
He scrambles for his thoughts across the headlines

recounts on stubby fingers the vices he declined[1]
the strain of sacrifice his children never held.

15 . . . But dazed by so much thought and recall
the ageing man keels over. Almost bent double, he's
anchored to his eggs.

[1] *declined* – turned away from

Silver Wedding

Vernon Scannell   *England*

The party is over and I sit among
The flotsam[1] that its passing leaves.
The dirty glasses and fag-ends:
Outside, a black wind grieves.

₅ Two decades and a half of marriage;
It does not really seem as long.
And yet I find I have scant knowledge
Of youth's ebullient² song.

David, my son, my loved rival,
₁₀ And Julia, my tapering daughter,
Now grant me one achievement only:
I turn their wine to water.

And Helen, partner of all these years,
Helen, my spouse, my sack of sighs,
₁₅ Reproaches me for every hurt
With injured, bovine³ eyes.

There must have been passion once, I grant,
But neither she nor I could bear
To have its ghost come prowling from
₂₀ Its dark and frowsy lair.

And we, to keep our nuptials⁴ warm,
Still wage sporadic, fire-side war;
Numb with insult each yet strives
To scratch the other raw.

₂₅ Twenty-five years we've now survived;
I'm not sure either why or how
As I sit with a wreath of quarrels set
On my tired and balding brow.

¹ *flotsam* – wreckage found floating
² *ebullient* – high-spirited
³ *bovine* – like a cow
⁴ *nuptials* – activities of a wedding or marriage

Earth is Brown
Shana Yardan *Guyana*

Earth is brown and rice is green,
And air is cold on the face of the soul

Oh grandfather, my grandfather,
your dhoti[1] is become a shroud
5 your straight hair a curse
in this land where
rice no longer fills the belly
or the empty placelessness
of your soul
10 For you cannot remember India.
The passage of time
has too long been trampled over
to bear your wistful[2] recollections.
and you only know the name
15 of the ship they brought you on
because your daadi told it to you.

Your sons with their city faces
don't know it at all
Don't want to know it.
20 Nor to understand that
you cannot cease
this communion with the smell
of cow-dung at fore-day morning,
′ or the rustling wail
25 of yellow-green rice
or the security of
mud between your toes
or the sensual[3] pouring
of paddy through your fingers.

30 Oh grandfather, my grandfather,
your dhoti is become a shroud.
Rice beds no longer call your sons.

They are clerks in the city of streets
Where life is a weekly paypacket
35 purchasing identity in Tiger Bay,[4]
seeking a tomorrow in today's unreality.
You are too old now to doubt
that Hannuman[5] hears you.
Yet outside your logie[6]
40 the fluttering cane
flaps like a plaintive tabla[7]
in the wind.
And when the spaces inside you
can no longer be filled
45 by the rank beds of rice,
and the lowering morning
cannot stir you to rise
from your ghoola.[8]
The music in your heart
50 will sound a rustling sound,
and the bamboos to Hannuman
will be a sitar[9] in the wind.

[1] *dhoti* – loin cloth wrapped round waist and hips
[2] *wistful* – regretful, sad
[3] *sensual* – giving pleasure to the senses
[4] *Tiger Bay* – in Georgetown, Guyana
[5] *Hannuman* – Hindu monkey god
[6] *logie* – hut
[7] *tabla* – pair of small hand drums
[8] *ghoola* – bed
[9] *sitar* – Indian stringed instrument

Those Winter Sundays
Robert Hayden   USA

Sundays too my father got up early
and put his clothes on in the blueblack cold,
then with cracked hands that ached
from labour in the weekday weather made
5 banked fires blaze. No one ever thanked him.

I'd wake and hear the cold splintering, breaking.
When the rooms were warm, he'd call,
and slowly I would rise and dress,
fearing the chronic¹ angers of that house,

10 Speaking indifferently to him,
who had driven out the cold
and polished my good shoes as well.
What did I know, what did I know
of love's austere² and lonely offices?

¹ *chronic* – going on for a long time, incurable
² *austere* – unfussy, self-denying, plain

Funeral Song
Olive Senior   *Jamaica*

You hide I'll come
seek you I'd cried
to a boy
like green
5 in a garden
but the flowers
that hide him
are planted too deep
the sky
10 they've appointed
his warden

I count sunflowers
hibiscus
and daisies
15 daisies
chrysanthemums
and roses
I'll be good
if you'll keep me

20 I'd said
   to the boy
   like life
   in the park
   but his lips
25 now are sealed
   and his eyes
   cannot open
   conscientia
   confused
30 with the dark

   I count sunflowers
   hibiscus
   and daisies
   daisies
35 chrysanthemums
   and roses.

Coffins
Cecil Gray   *Trinidad and Tobago*

Coffins were simple things – plain planes of wood
varnished over, cornered together and glued
at the shoulders. The handles, though, shone
mock gold or silver, spiralled[1] for the grip.

5 Undertakers used to come to the house
with an ice-box to stand in the centre
of the room. Friends of the home, some neighbours
and people they knew circled its window
saying 'Only yesterday we . . .', claiming
10 'It was a sign that she knew she was going.'

And wakes were rituals² with strong, black
coffee and crackers served to card-players
and singers of hymns. Waves of wailing rose
and slowly ebbed. Bouts of staccato³ sobs
15　broke out. Reminiscences,⁴ like the candles
in corners, brightened the name of the dead.

My mother's going was not mourned like that.
She lay unvisited, berthed⁵ and labelled
in a strange, locked cabin; not centred in
20　candles and weeping. Later we placed her
in a plain, simple box and followed it,
anger's iron hardening the lips of my grief.

Till death I will circle again, again,
the oval I looked into framing her face,
25　her last smile wise with pardon, her closed eyes
my blindness that kept me turned from her pain.

¹ *spiralled* – like a screw
² *rituals* – things done in a customary way
³ *staccato* – jerky
⁴ *reminiscences* – tales of past events
⁵ *berthed* – placed in a space

Mid-term Break
Seamus Heaney　*Ireland*

I sat all morning in the college sick bay
Counting bells knelling classes to a close.
At two o'clock our neighbours drove me home.
In the porch I met my father crying –
5　He had always taken funerals in his stride –
And Big Jim Evans saying it was a hard blow.

The baby cooed and laughed and rocked the pram
When I came in, and I was embarrassed
By old men standing up to shake my hand

10 And tell me they were 'sorry for my trouble'.
Whispers informed strangers I was the eldest,
Away at school, as my mother held my hand

In hers and coughed out angry tearless sighs.
At ten o'clock the ambulance arrived
15 With the corpse, stanched[1] and bandaged by the nurses.

Next morning I went up into the room. Snowdrops
And candles soothed the bedside; I saw him
For the first time in six weeks. Paler now,

Wearing a poppy bruise on his left temple,
20 He lay in the four foot box as in his cot.
No gaudy[2] scars, the bumper[3] knocked him clear.

A four foot box, a foot for every year.

[1] *stanched* – kept from bleeding
[2] *gaudy* – brightly coloured
[3] *bumper* – part of a car

A Visit to Jamaica and a Walk Through Kingston
James Berry   *Jamaica*

My peripheral eye[1] caught
familiar angles. I knew he hid
with the waiting people
of the city's backland.

5 My steps halted,
in joy in fear,
beside a bowed wreck.

It was busily suspicious face,
something seldom aroused,
10 the clothes a stink nest.
My memory sharpened the jolly
stutterer at school.

My anxious voice bounced loose
like an old embrace of boyhood.
15 Leo, man! I said.

A glare unlidded his old
froggy eyes. A rush of memory opened
his mouth and arms. A twist
hardened a contemptuous² mouth
20 in a knotted beard.

He slowly drew a final door.
It seemed my voice,
my dress, my look, wounded him
as if I was a foreign reporter,
25 to expose him, to say

he chickened out on his children.
His word staggering manhood
had linked his first girl, I knew.
He had sustained a fluency
30 of eight new lives. I knew
he had left them, years now.

But I knew him before all that.
Leo! My voice pulled
at his hurried and ragged turn away.
35 My early village friend was armless
and wordless for me.

Was this the final man?
There was no joke,
no touch.

40 Leo! I whispered.
His shuffles mounted
a wider and wider distance.

¹ *peripheral eye* – *peripheral vision* – is the extreme left and right of what you
  can see – what you see 'out of the corner of your eye'
² *contemptuous* – scornful

Brothers
Michael Longley *Ireland*

I was a mother and a father to him
Once his pebble spectacles had turned cloudy
And his walk slowed to a chair by the fire.
Often I would come back from herding sheep
5 Or from the post office with our pensions
To find his darkness in darkness, the turf[1]
Shifting ashes on to last flakes of light.
The room was made more silent by the flies
That circled the soup stains on his waistcoat.
10 The dog preferred to curl up under his hand
And raced ahead as soon as I neared the lane.
I read to him from one of his six books,
Thick pages dropping from the broken spines
Of *Westward Ho!* and *The Children's Reciter.*
15 Sometimes I pulled faces, and he didn't know,
Or I paraded naked in front of him
As though I was looking in a mirror.
Two neighbours came visiting after he died.
Mad[2] for the learning, a character, they said
20 And awakened in me a pride of sorts.
I picture his hand when I stroke the dog,
His legs if I knock the kettle from the hearth.
It's his peculiar way of putting things
That fills in the spaces of Tullabaun.[3]
25 The dregs stewed in the teapot remind me
And wind creaming rainwater off the butt.[4]

[1] *turf* – peat used for fuel, to keep fires
[2] *mad* – very enthusiatic, funny
[3] *Tullabaun* – a place in Ireland
[4] *butt* – a barrel for collecting rainwater

The Misses Norman

Cecil Gray   *Trinidad and Tobago*

The Misses Norman lived on Marine Square
just as you turn from Broadway at the corner
where now a granite[1] bank shines like new coins;
two short white matrons that I remember
5 like Lord's Prayers on a rosary that joins
a knotted childhood to their acts of care.

To my young mind it seemed a threatening place.
You pierced the wooden gate through its small door
and stepped into a dimness armed with plants,
10 cringed up the half-gloom to the upper floor
and called good morning nervous in your pants.
But there you spoke with goodness face to face.

With thanks now rising in me like a lake
an image flashes fresh as yesterday;
15 a slippered sister in Edwardian dress
shuffling to hear each stanza of distress,
bribing the waiting teeth of reefs away.
It is a bonding that time cannot break.

The lifeguards of this heaving world are rare,
20 the sinking swimmers thick as August rain.
But one whose feet touched safely when that pair
of spinsters anchored themselves to pain
that was not theirs attempts a line of praise
in words like them, as faithful and as plain.

[1] *granite* – a hard stone like marble

Discussion and Activities

When Folks Like You have Birthdays p83

1 Why do you suppose the 'I' said 'the country should fire a 21-gun salute' (l 2)? Why 'we thought of you' (l 22)?

2 What was happening in Kingston on the 'you's' birthday? Which guns were firing (l 15) do you think? What 'shouting was heard' (l 16)? Whose 'whistles were blown' (l 17)? Why do you suppose they 'had a curfew' (l 15)?

3 How do you interpret 'the new breaks through' (l 11)? How effective as a metaphor is 'the old, hard crust' (l 10) do you think? (Remember a metaphor is used to make the meaning of what is being said more memorable for the reader to imagine. The best metaphors are those that are fresh and original, never or hardly used before.)

4 What part does *contrast* play in the poem? Does it do anything to increase the feeling of regret in the tone or does it only bring the poem more down to earth?

For My Mother p84

1 How did the mother meet the father for the first time? Was he really 'from a country/one hundred miles south of hers' (l 7-8)? What would you say drew her to him? In what ways were they different? Which special features of the wedding impressed the people of Harvey River, Hanover? What was her face 'washed by' (l 40)? In the marriage, what did she have to do to help to support the family? How was that different from what her parents expected? How did she show devotion to her children?

2 Explain as well as you can what you take each of these phrases to mean: 'her fate disguised' (l 5)' 'my blue-eyed grandmother' (l 15); 'sure in the kingdom' (l 15); 'combed Jewlit backstreets' (l 29); 'it was a brazen bride in those days' (l 35); 'the unknown of her belly' (l 38); 'a span that defied time' (l 49); 'the perpetual quality of wonder' (l 56).

3 What stereotyped image of West Indian men is suggested in 'my father whom all women loved' (l 56)? How do you interpret 'hurt his bride' (l 57)? Who do you suppose was 'this 'Friend' who stood by

her side' (l 58)? Can you think why the mother was 'adamant' (l 59)?
How does 'straight-backed' (l 62) help you in understanding why the
mother remained 'dry-eyed' (l 63) when her husband died? When did
she break down and cry? Lines 70-74 tell what she cried over. What
were they? How would you interpret 'the pain she bore with the eyes
of a queen' (l 74)? To what extent would you suggest this mother
represents mothers of the West Indies?

4 What kind of tone of voice do you hear in the words of the 'I' in the
poem? How would you describe the attitude of the speaker? Try to
describe the feeling the poem leaves you with and suggest how the
poet made the poem communicate that feeling.

Pa p87

1 The 'Guardian' (l 3) is a copy of the *Trinidad Guardian* newspaper.
Why is it said to be 'drooling from his hands' (l 3)? How is he
sitting? Why are 'scrambled eggs' (l 2) there? What do you take
'kneels over' (l 18) to mean? How did he get 'anchored to his eggs'
(l 19)?

2 'he concludes' (l 5). What does he conclude about when he had
'sharp two-toned shoes' (l 7)? When did he have 'steady hands'
(l 8)? Do you take 'he rolled and pitched the seas with the best'
(l 11) to mean he was a sailor, or as another metaphor? Say why.
If you take it literally say why.

3 What do you imagine were 'the corner stones of his world'
(ll 12-13)? What do you suppose was his 'fixed drive' (l 13)? Was it
related to 'the strain of sacrifice his children never held' (l 16)? If so,
how? Why did he decline vices?

4 In what way is this poem similar to *Those Winter Sundays* (p90)
and in which ways different?

Silver Wedding p87

1 What was 'The party' for? Who are the people mentioned and
what is said about each? What do you think the speaker means in
line 12?

2 Explain what you think lines 7-8 are saying. Which 'ghost' is meant
in line 19? Who does not want that 'ghost' to return? What then
has gone out of the marriage? What is described in lines 22-24?
Who 'reproaches' (l 15) whom and for what? Do you think the

speaker also reproaches? How is that related to 'a wreath of quarrels' (l 27)? Do you have any experience of two people behaving that way?

3 Which one or more of these is the speaker expressing: a) regret; b) relief; c) resignation; d) anger; e) boredom; f) bitterness; g) sorrow? Why do you suppose he says 'a black wind grieves' (l 4)? 'Twenty-five years we've now survived' (l 25). What does that mean? How do you account for the survival? In your experience could two people who love each other 'scratch the other raw' (l 24)? How do you imagine such a relationship is different from adolescent romantic love?

4 One of the metaphors or comparisons the poet has used is 'flotsam' (l 2). It is a comparison that has been used many times before. Choose three or four other metaphors and consider how fresh and original each is, and how effective in impressing an idea in your mind.

Earth is Brown p89

1 People from India were brought to the West Indies and Guyana as indentured labourers from 1838 to 1924. What has 'the passage of time' (l 11) done to the grandfather? Which 'recollections' (l 13) do you think were meant? What do you think 'the empty placelessness of your soul' (ll 8-9) has to do with 'For you cannot remember India' (l 10)?

2 What is it the sons 'with their city faces' (l 17) don't want to know' (l 19)? What do you suppose they think of the grandfather's employment compared with theirs? What do they not want to understand? Why is the phrase 'this communion' (l 22) used?

3 'Hanuman' (l 37), the monkey god, is an aspect of God in the Hindu religion. What do you suppose the grandfather thinks he 'hears' (l 38)? How do the canes remind him of tabla (small hand-drums)? When, do you imagine, 'the morning will not stir him to rise from his ghoola-bed' (l 48)? What does the speaker in the poem think he will hear? How do you interpret 'your dhoti is become a shroud' (l 4, 31)? (A dhoti is a cloth Hindu men wrap around themselves)

4 Which of these would you say this poem is about? Could it be about more than one? Give your reasons. a) how people forget things; b) changing times; c) the life of a farmer; d) not fitting into a place.

5 Compare this poem with The *Saddhu of Couva* (p207).

Those Winter Sundays p90

1 Is there any reason you can see why the father 'made banked fires blaze' (ll 4-5)? How easy was it for him to do? What connection could there be between 'No one ever thanked him' (l 5) and 'the chronic (habitual) angers of that house' (l 9)? Who do you imagine carried 'chronic angers'? Beside making the fire, what else did the 'I' say the father did?

2 'What did I know, what did I know' (l 13). What is the 'I' saying about himself there? What did he not know about? Why, do you imagine, did he not know? Did he ever know at all?

3 'offices' (l 14) means jobs to be done. Why are they described as 'austere' (without joy or pleasure) and 'lonely'? What has 'love' to do with them? What do you imagine the speaker is feeling about his father in the poem?

4 In what way is the poem similar to *Pa* (p87)?

Funeral Song p91

1 How soon in the poem do you realise the boy has died? What is the 'I' remembering about him?

2 Flowers are things that give people pleasure. Why are they used in the poem in contrast with what happened to the boy? Would you say there is some irony in the poem that the 'I' is telling about? Explain why or why not.

Coffins p92

1 What do you take to be 'the oval I looked into framing her face' (l 24)? Why do you suppose the 'I' speaks of 'anger's iron hardening the lips of my grief' (l 22)?

2 When are wakes held? According to the speaker in the poem, what usually happened at wakes? Which metaphors are used in telling about wakes? Why did the 'I' say 'my mother's going was not mourned like that' (l 17)?

3 What feeling, if any, comes to you from 'not centred in candles and weeping' (ll 19-20), 'She lay unvisited' (l 18), and 'in a strange locked cabin' (l 19)?

4 Why do you suppose the 'I' says 'I will circle again, again' (l 23)? Is his mother still there? What does the last line of the poem reveal? What thoughts and feelings do you imagine going through

him now? If the poem succeeded in communicating any strong
feeling to you, try to identify what it is in the poem that does
that.

Mid-Term Break p93

1 'the bumper knocked him clear' (l 21). Which bumper? Knocked
   whom? When? How old was he? What had made 'a poppy bruise
   on his left temple' (l 19)?
2 Why do you think the 'I' was taken from class and 'sat all morning
   in the college sick bay' (l 1)? Whom did he meet when he was
   taken home? Why did the 'I' say 'He had always taken funerals in
   his stride' (l 5)? What embarrassed the 'I'? What was the 'hard blow'
   (l 6)?
3 How do you think the mother felt as she 'coughed out angry
   tearless sighs' (l 13)? The 'I' does not say that he cried. How do you
   imagine he felt? Why did he not cry?
4 Twice in the poem there is something in *contrast* with the scene
   around. Where are those contrasts? How do they serve to deepen
   what was happening in the house?

A Visit to Jamaica and a Walk Through Kingston p94

1   Who or what was the 'bowed wreck' (l 7)? Why did the 'I' say 'in
   joy in fear' (l 6)? What do you imagine from 'a stink nest' (l 10)?
2 'My memory sharpened' (l 11). What came to mind? Why was the
   'I's voice 'anxious' (l 13)? How do you interpret 'A rush of memory
   opened his mouth and arms' (ll 17-18)? What seemed to be the
   reason or reasons why 'A twist hardened a contemptuous mouth'
   (l 19) Have you ever seen someone behave like that out of shame?
   What had Leo done with his life? Was that related, do you think, to
   'My early village friend was armless and wordless for me' (ll 35-36)?
3 Do you find the incident funny or tragic? Say why.

Brothers p96

1 What does the 'I' mean by 'I was a mother and a father to him' (l 1)?
   Find four places where a reader is told that the 'he' could not see.
   How do you see him in your imagination?
2 The neighbours said the 'he' was 'mad for the learning'
   (l 19) meaning he wanted to learn things that were in books. Why

do you think they said that? Why, then, did they call him 'a character' (l 19), meaning an unusual person? Why do you suppose that awakened in the 'I' 'a pride of sorts' (l 20)?

3 What is the feeling you get from lines 21-26? What then was the poem written to express?

The Misses Norman p97

1 What 'seemed a threatening place' (l 7)? Who lived there? What is there now? Who did 'acts of care' (l 6)? What do you take 'a knotted childhood' (l 6) to mean?

2 How do you interpret 'spoke with goodness face to face' (l 12)? Why do you think the 'I' says 'thanks now rising in me like a lake' (l 13)? Thanks for what? Thanks to whom? What do you think are described as 'the waiting teeth of reefs' (l 17)? Who are called 'lifeguards' (l 19)?

3 Use is made of metaphors to communicate the meaning of the poem. Consider some of them and form an opinion about the effectiveness of each one, i.e. how it helps you to grasp something and to stamp it on your mind.

4 The writer has used rhyme at the ends of certain lines. In the first stanza the scheme or pattern is ABCBCA. Plot out the rhyme scheme for each of the other stanzas and say whether they are all similar or different.

Fuss-pot
Ian McDonald   *Trinidad and Tobago*

The old woman never stopped complaining:
It seemed her sign of life, her signature.
The food was bad or salt or made her sick,
Water had the bitter taste of aloes in her mouth,
5 Bed was hard or full of lumps or flea-infested,
The light was bad, mosquitoes stung her toes,
The place was hot or cold, whichever was most trouble,
And she never got the right amount of good attention.
And whenever the children visited, she let them have her tongue.

10 She deserved the suck-teeth she all the time received.
Strange, then, at the end, when agony came on,
She was calm and quiet as the day is long.
Lay back and never made a single petty call
And seemed to try and find a deepening peace within.
15 And when the children came you noted, with surprise,
How close they clung to her with many signs of love.

Who can delve into all the years gone by?
All one can tell is in behaviour now.
She takes on strength and certainty and love,
20 She summons seriousness in place of spite.
Death for her is drama worth her while
Too big, it seems, to make a fuss about.

This is the Dark Time my Love
Martin Carter   *Guyana*

This is the dark time, my love.
All round the land brown beetles crawl about.
The shining sun is hidden in the sky.
Red flowers bend their heads in awful sorrow.

5 This is the dark time, my love.
It is the season of oppression,[1] dark metal, and tears.
It is the festival of guns, the carnival of misery.
Everywhere the faces of men are strained and anxious.

Who comes waiting in the dark night time?
10 Whose boot of steel tramps down the slender grass?
It is the man of death, my love, the strange invader
watching you sleep and aiming at your dream.

[1] *oppression* – unjust government

We are the Women
Lorna Goodison *Jamaica*

We are the women
with thread bags
anchored deep in our bosoms
containing blood agreements
5 silver coins and cloves of garlic
and an apocrypha.[1]
of Nanny's secrets.

We've made peace
with want
10 if it doesn't kill us
we'll live with it.
We ignore promises
of plenty
we know that old sankey.[2]

15 We are the ones
who are always waiting
mouth corner white
by sepulchres[3] and
bone yards

20 for the bodies of our men,
   waiting under massa
   waiting under massa table
   for the trickle down of crumbs.

   We are the women
25 who ban our bellies
   with strips from the full moon
   our nerves made keen
   from hard grieving
   worn thin like
30 silver sixpences.

   We've buried our hope
   too long
   as the anchor to our
   navel strings
35 we are rooting at
   the burying spot
   we are uncovering
   our hope.

[1] *apocrypha* – false account
[2] *sankey* – story, explanation
[3] *sepulchres* – tombs

Ballad of Birmingham
Dudley Randall   USA

"Mother dear, may I go downtown
Instead of out to play,
and march the streets of Birmingham
in a freedom march today?"

5 "No, baby, no, you may not go,
for the dogs are fierce and wild,
and clubs and hoses, guns and jails
ain't good for a little child."

"But, mother, I won't be alone.
10 Other children will go with me,
and march the streets of Birmingham
to make our country free."

"No, baby, no, you may not go,
for I fear those guns will fire.
15 But you may go to church instead,
and sing in the children's choir."

She has combed and brushed her nightdark hair,
and bathed rose petal sweet,
and drawn white gloves on her small brown hands,
20 and white shoes on her feet.

The mother smiled to know her child
was in the sacred place,
but that smile was the last smile
to come upon her face.

25 For when she heard the explosion,
her eyes grew wet and wild.
She raced through the streets of Birmingham
calling for her child.

She clawed through bits of glass and brick,
30 then lifted out a shoe.
"O, here's the shoe my baby wore,
but, baby, where are you?"

The Emigrants
Edward Brathwaite   *Barbados*

So you have seen them
with their cardboard grips,[1]
felt hats, rain-
cloaks, the women

5 with their plain
or purple-tinted
coats hiding their fatten-
ed hips.

These are the Emigrants.
10 On sea-port quays
at air ports
anywhere where there is ship
or train, swift
motor car, or jet
15 to travel faster than the breeze
you see them gathered:
passports stamped
their travel papers wrapped
in old disused news-
20 papers: lining their patient queues.
Where to?
They do not know.
Canada, the Panama
Canal, the Miss-
25 issippi painfields, Florida?
Or on to dock,
at hissing smoke locked
Glasgow?

Why do they go?
30 They do not know.
Seeking a job
they settle for the very best
the agent has to offer:
jabbing a neighbour
35 out of work for four bob[2]
less a week.

What do they hope for
what find there
these New World mariners[3]
40 Columbus coursing kaffirs[4]

What Cathay⁵ shores
for them are gleaming golden
what magic keys they carry to unlock
what gold endragoned doors?

¹ *grips* – suitcases
² *bob* – shillings, English money
³ *mariners* – sailors
⁴ *kaffirs* – those of the Xhosa tribes of S. Africa, but used by whites there to be insulting
⁵ *Cathay* – what China was called when Europeans sought its riches

Soil

R.S. Thomas   *Wales*

A field with tall hedges and a young
Moon in the branches and one star
Declining westward set the scene
Where he works slowly astride the rows
Of red mangolds and green swedes¹
Plying mechanically his cold blade.

5 This is his world, the hedge defines
The mind's limits; only the sky
Is boundless, and he never looks up;
His gaze is deep in the dark soil,
As are his feet. The soil is all;
His hands fondle it, and his bones
10 Are formed out of it with the swedes.
And if sometimes the knife errs,
Burying itself in his shocked flesh,
Then out of the wound the blood seeps home
To the warm soil from which it came.

15

¹ *swede* – a root vegetable

A Black Man Talks of Reaping

Arna Bontemps   *USA*

I have sown beside all waters in my day.
I planted deep, within my heart the fear
that wind or fowl would take the grain away.
I planted safe against this stark,[1] lean year.
5 I scattered seed enough to plant the land
in rows from Canada to Mexico
but for my reaping only what the hand
can hold at once is all that I can show.

Yet what I sowed and what the orchard yields
10 my brother's sons are gathering stalk and root;
small wonder then my children glean in fields
they have not sown, and feed on bitter fruit.

[1] *stark* – bare
[2] *glean* – to gather grain from a field after it has been harvested

Maljo's Political Party (from *Omeros*)

Derek Walcott   *St Lucia*

By the witness of flambeaux-bottles, by the sweat
of distorted[1] faces screaming for Workers' Rights
on the steps of the iron market, Philoctete

peered at each candidate through the blinding arc-lights
5 to cresting gusts of applause for an island torn
by identical factions: one they called Marxist,

led by the barber's son, the other by Compton
which Maljo, who took him there, called Capitalist.
In the rumshop he asked Maljo which to support.

10 "Me," Maljo said, "them two men fighting for one bone."
He'd pay his deposit,[2] he'd rent Hector's transport
and buy batteries for a hand-held megaphone.

His party was launched at the depot. The ribbon
was cut by the priest, its pieces saved for later
15 Christmas presents. In the village where he was born,

a tall cynic[3] heckled: "Scissors can't cut water!"
"Ciseau pas ça couper de l'eau!" meaning the campaign
was a wasted effort; the candidate addressed

his barefoot followers with a glass of champagne
20 to toast their trust, and a megaphone which he pressed
for its crackling echo, deafening those two feet

away from him. Since every party cost money,
he marched his constituents[4] clapping up the street
to the No Pain Café to start the ceremony.

25 There Seven Seas sang for them, there his good compére[5]
Achille promised to canvas[6] for him in the depot
during domino games. A new age would begin.

You could read its poster by the sodium glow
of a lamppost at night. Its insomniac[7] grin
30 plastered on a moonlit wall with its cheering surf,

while the charter yachts slept and crabs counted the sand,
with his registered name: F. DIDIER, BORN TO SERVE,
its sign: a broken chain dangling from a black hand.

"Bananas shall raise their hands at the oppressor,
35 through all our valleys!" he screamed, forgetting to press
the megaphone button. They named him "Professor

Static," or "Statics," for short, the short-circuit prose
of his electrical syntax[8] in which he mixed
Yankee and patois as the lethargic[9] Comet

40 sputtered its sparked broadsides when the button was fixed.
As Party Distributor he paid Philoctete,
who limped in the vanguard[10] with handouts while the crowd

shouted "Statics!" and Maljo waved. He, who was once
fisherman-mechanic, felt newly empowered
45 to speak for those at the backs of streets, all the ones

idling in breadfruit yards, or draping the bridges
at dusk by the clogged drains, or hanging tired nets
on tired bamboo, for shacks on twilight ridges

in the wounding dusk. Their patience was Philoctete's.
50 By the Comet's symbol he knew their time had come.
and what Philo could contribute as a member

was the limp that drove his political point home
as he hopped to Maljo's funeral timbre,[11]
haranguing[12] the back streets, forgetting the button.

[1] *distorted* – twisted
[2] *deposit* – money paid to register a candidate which is returned if he/she wins
a certain number of votes
[3] *cynic* – a person who doubts bad can be turned to good
[4] *constituents* – those who could vote for him
[5] *compère* – friend
[6] *canvas* – seek voters
[7] *insomniac* – unsleeping
[8] *syntax* – language, grammar
[9] *lethargic* – slow, lazy
[10] *vanguard* – front
[11] *timbre* – tone
[12] *haranguing* – making speeches to, calling out at

Sometimes in the Middle of the Story
for the drowned Africans of the Middle Passage
Edward Baugh   Jamaica

Sometimes in the middle of the story something
move outside the house, like
it could be the wind, but is not the wind
and the story-teller hesitate so slight
5 you hardly notice it, and the children
hold their breath and look at one another.

The old people say is Toussaint passing
on his grey horse Bel-Argent, moving
faster than backra-massa[1] timepiece
10 know to measure, briefing[2] the captains
setting science and strategy to trap the emperor.
But also that sound had something in it
of deep water, salt water, had ocean
the sleep-sigh of a drowned African
15 turning in his sleep on the ocean floor
and Toussaint horse was coming from far
his tail trailing the swish of the sea
from secret rendezvous,[3] from councils of war
with those who never completed the journey,
20 and we below deck heard only the muffled
thud of scuffling feet, could only
guess the quick, fierce tussle, the
stifled gasp, the barrel-chests bursting
the bubbles rising and breaking, the blue
25 closing over. But their souls shuttle
still the forest paths of ocean
connecting us still the current unbroken
the circuits kept open, the tireless messengers
the ebony princes of your lost Atlantis[4]
30 a power of black men rising from the sea.

[1] *backra massa* – white overseer or master
[2] *briefing* – telling or explaining
[3] *rendezvous* – a place agreed on to meet
[4] *Atlantis* – the land that sank and is now the north Atlantic Ocean

Tom
Edward Brathwaite   *Barbados*

Under the burnt out green
of this small yard's
tufts of grass
where water was once used
5 to wash pots, pans, poes,

ochre appears. A rusted
bucket, hole kicked into its
bottom, lies on its side.

Fence, low wall of careful
10 stones marking the square
yard, is broken now, breached
by pigs, by rats, by mongoose
and by neighbours. Eucalyptus
bushes push their way amidst
15 the marl.[1] All looks so left
so unlived in: yard, fence and cabin.

Here old Tom lived: his whole
tight house no bigger than your
sitting room. Here was his world
20 banged like a fist on broken
chairs, bare table and the side-
board dresser where he kept his cups.
One wooden only door, still latched,
hasp broken; one window, wooden,
25 broken: four slats still intact.[2]
Darkness pours from these wrecked boards
and from the crab torn spaces underneath the door.

These are the deepest reaches of time's long
attack. The roof, dark shingles,
30 silvered in some places by the wind, the finger-
tips of weather, shines still secure, still
perfect, although the plaster peels from walls,
at sides, at back, from high up near the roof: in places
where it was not painted. But from the front,
35 the face from which it looked out on the world,
the house retains its lemon wash as smooth and bland as pearl.

But the tide creeps in: today's
insistence laps the loneliness of this
resisting cabin: the village grows and bulges:
40 shops, super-

markets, Postal Agency
whose steel-spectacled mistress
rules the town. But no one knows
where Tom's cracked limestone oblong lies.
45 The house, the Postal Agent says,
is soon to be demolished:
a Housing Estate's being spawned[3]
to feel the greedy town.

No one
50 knows Tom now, no one cares.
Slave's days are past, forgotten. The faith, the dream denied,
the things he dared
not do, all lost, if un-
55 forgiven. This house is all
that's left of hopes, of hurt,
of history . . .

[1] *marl* – soil
[2] *intact* – whole
[3] *spawned* – given birth

Hill Houses
Barnabas J. Ramon-Fortuné *Trinidad and Tobago*

Huddle of houses on the hillslope
Like animals huddled together
Upon a tether[1] of hope.

Huddled together as small fears
5 Flock together for safety
when large danger nears.

Rickety, falling-apart houses
Patched and patched again
Like a beggar's trousers,

10 Holding against the wind's claws,
    The elephant-hoofed rain,
    And furtive² age that gnaws

    At the worn, crumbling pillars,
    The one-hinge, one-nail doors,
15 Frail, yet strong as the dwellers

    That live in these shacks on the hillslope,
    If, in a moment of weakness,
    Their ragged, skeletal hope

20 Ever should fail to support them,
    They will come tumbling headlong
    Down the slope like flotsam,³

    Floorboards, windows, doors,
    Tossing, tumbling, flying
    From the wind's murderous claws,

25 The thundering hooves of the rain,
    And left after heartless plunder
    Strewn from the hill to the plain,

    And the folk from the murdered hill,
    Borne down in the wreck of their hope,
30 Lie quiet and broken and still,

    And their hearts, when the rage has abated⁴
    Like the hill, lie naked and bare
    And utterly devastated,⁵

    That never a stone or a tear
35 Ever shall rise like a tower
    Out of the ruins of fear.

¹ *tether* – a rope used to stop an animal from wandering away
² *furtive* – sly, cunning, secretive
³ *flotsam* – wreckage or rubbish found floating on the sea
⁴ *abated* – got less severe
⁵ *devastated* – destroyed

In My Fourteenth Year (from *Another Life*)

Derek Walcott   *St Lucia*

About the August of my fourteenth year
I lost my self somewhere above a valley
owned by a spinster-farmer, my dead father's friend.
At the hill's edge there was a scarp[1]
5   with bushes and boulders stuck in its side.
Afternoon light ripped the valley,
rifling smoke climbed from small labourers' houses,
and I dissolved into a trance.
I was seized by a pity more profound[2]
10 than my young body could bear, I climbed
with the labouring smoke,
I drowned in labouring breakers of bright cloud,
then uncontrollably I began to weep,
inwardly, without tears, with a serene extinction[3]
15 of all sense; I felt compelled to kneel,
I wept for nothing and for everything,
I wept for the earth of the hill under my knees,
for the grass, the pebbles, for the cooking smoke
above the labourers' houses like a cry,
20 for unheard avalanches[4] of white cloud,
but "darker grows the valley, more and more forgetting."
For their lights still shine through the hovels like litmus,
the smoking lamp still slowly says its prayer,
the poor still move behind their tinted scrim,[5]
25 the taste of water is still shared everywhere,
but in that ship of night, locked in together,
through which, like chains, a little light might leak,
something still fastens us forever to the poor.

[1] *scarp* – slope of a ravine
[2] *profound* – deep
[3] *extinction* – blanking out
[4] *avalanches* – slides of snow
[5] *scrim* – transparent curtain

To the Madwoman in my Yard
Olive Senior   *Jamaica*

Lady: please don't throw rocks at my window
because this is Holy House and God send you
to get all the moneylenders out drive the harlot
from the inner temple. Again. Please don't
5 creep up behind me when I'm gardening beg me
lend you a knife. A bucket. A rope. Hope. Then
threaten to ignite, set alight and consume me
for you are the Daughter-of-a-Eunuch-and-a-Firefly
sent to X-ray and exhume me.

10 Lady: this is nonsense. Here I am trying hard
with my Life. With Society. You enter my yard
dressed like furies or bats. Bring right in to me
all the hell I've been trying to escape from.
Thought a Barbican gate could hold in the
15 maelstrom. Keep out the Dungle. And bats.

What you want? Bring me down to your level?
 – A life built on scraps. A fretwork of memory
which is garbage. A jungle of images: parson
and hellfire all that's sustaining. The childhood
20 a house built of straw could not stand. The man
like a roach on the walls. So you choose
out of doors. Or my garden.

Lady: as you rant and you shout, threaten
and cajole me, seek me out then debar me
25 you don't move me one blast: Life Equals Control.

Yes. Here is what the difference betwen us
is about. I wear my madness in. You wear yours out.

A Storm Passes (from *Omeros*)
Derek Walcott *St Lucia*

In the devastated[1] valleys, crumpling brown water
at their prows,[2] headlights on, passenger-vans floated
slowly up roads that were rivers, through the slaughter
of the years' banana-crop, past stiff cows bloated[3]
5 from engorging[4] mud as the antlers[5] of trees tossed
past the banks like migrating elk.[6] It was as if

the rivers, envying the sea, tired of being crossed
in one leap, had joined in a power so massive
that it made islands of villages, made bridges

10 the sieves[7] of a force that shouldered culverts aside.
The rain passed, but people looked up to the ridges
fraying[8] with its return, and the flood, in its pride,

entered the sea; then Achille could hear the tunnels
of brown water roaring in the mangroves; its tide
15 hid the keels of the canoes, and their wet gunwales[9]

were high with rainwater that could warp them rotten
if they were not bailed. The river was satisfied.
It was a god too. Too much had been forgotten.

Then, a mouse after a fête, its claws curled like moss,
20 nosing the dew as the lighthouse opened its eye,
the sunlight peeped out, and people surveyed the loss

that the gods had made under a clearing-up sky.
Candles shortened and died. The big yellow tractors
tossed up the salad of trees, in yellow jackets
25 men straightened the chairs of dead poles, the contractors
in white helmets and slickers heard the castanets[10]
of the waves going up the islands, moving on

from here to Guadeloupe, the beaded wires were still.
They saw the mess the gods made in one night alone,
30 as Lightning lifted his stilts[11] over the last hill.

Achille bailed out his canoe under an almond
that shuddered with rain. There would be brilliant days still,
till the next storm, and their freshness was wonderful.

[1] *devastated* – suffering destruction
[2] *prows* – bows of ships
[3] *bloated* – swollen
[4] *engorging* – swallowing
[5] *antlers* – horns
[6] *elk* – a kind of deer
[7] *sieves* – strainers
[8] *fraying* – losing edges, usually used of cloth
[9] *gunwales* – edges of the sides of boats
[10] *castanets* – pieces of wood held and clicked together
[11] *stilts* – tall poles used for walking on

Discussion and Activities

1 Why do you think complaining was called the 'sign of life' in the patient of this poem? Say what she complained about. What does 'suck-teeth' (l 10) mean? Who do you think did it? Why do you suppose it was said that 'She deserved the suck-teeth she all the time received' (l 10)?

2 What changes occurred when the agony of the end came on? How did the children seem to feel then when they came to see her? Explain as well as you can what you understand by line 20.

3 What reason does the speaker in the poem suggest why her fussy, dramatic behaviour stopped? Which drama took its place? Which of these would you agree is nearest to what the poem is saying? Say why. a) fussy people usually get tired b) bad patients pay for their disagreeableness c) the coming of death makes all else trivial d) when death approaches a person gets composed and ready e) some people just can't help being fussy.

This Is The Dark Time My Love p104

1 This poem was written when freedom in British Guiana was 'suspended' in 1953 and British soldiers policed the country. People were demanding social change and political independence. It was claimed that red communism was taking hold. Which line in the second stanza tells why it was 'the dark time'? Who is referred to as 'the stranger invader' (l 11)?

2 What do you imagine these to be? – 'brown beetles' (l 2); 'dark metal' (l 6); 'boot of steel' (l 10); 'the slender grass' (l 10). Who is referred to as 'the man of death' (l 11)? Why do you imagine the faces of men were 'strained and anxious' (l 8)?

3 What do you think the speaker means by line 3? Who were the 'Red flowers' (l 4)? Why did they 'bend their heads in awful sorrow' (l 4)? Which dream do you suppose is meant by 'your dream' (l 12)? How do you know that the movements of people were controlled? What comes to mind when you read 'the festival of guns' (l 7); 'the carnival of misery' (l 7)? What do you suppose the guns were used for?

4 'The shining sun' is a symbol for something else. What is it a symbol of? Which other symbols and metaphors do you recognise in the poem?

We Are the Women p105

1 What impressions do you get about the women? What do you think 'thread bags' (l 2) are? Say what you understand by 'We've made peace with want' (ll 8-9)? What is the 'old sankey' – old trickster's tale (l 14)? Why do you suppose they are 'the women who ban (band) their bellies' (ll 24-25)? Point to other places in the poem which impress you with the kind of life the women have.

2 An apocrypha is a book containing tales of doubtful truth. When you think of coins and garlic in the thread bags, what do you suppose is 'an apocrypha of Nanny's secrets' (ll 6-7)? Why do they need such an apocrypha?

3 How do lines 31-38 change the course of the poem? What, then, do you suppose the poem was written to say? Show how the images in lines 1-30 make the last 4 lines hearten us, raise our spirits.

Ballad of Birmingham p106

1 On Sunday, September 15, 1963, during the years when black Americans staged marches to get their rights, a dynamite bomb exploded in a black church in a town called Birmingham in Alabama. Four children were killed. What did the 'I' of the poem want to do that Sunday? What was the mother's response?

2 Where did the 'I' then go? The mother smiled (l 21). Why? What then made her race 'through the streets of Birmingham' (l 27)? What did she find? What does 'clawed' make you image?

3 A ballad is a story song. Do you think the poet wrote the poem just to tell a story, or for some other reason? Say why you think so.

4 What gives the poem heavy irony (a contradictory result)? How does that ironic twist give more force to the poem?

The Emigrants p107

1 A grip, you might know, is a suitcase. Why do the 'them' have grips? Why, do you think, are the suitcases of cardboard? Why are they 'The Emigrants'? Where would you 'see them gathered' (l 16)? Why?

2 Why do you think the speaker says 'They do not know' (l 22)? What do they really not know? Why are the five different places mentioned? Why does the speaker say 'the Mississippi painfields' (ll 24-25) instead of the Mississippi canefields? What is he suggesting about the state of Mississippi, in the southern USA,

where some West Indians go for a time every year as migrant labourers?

3 'they settle' (l 32). What does 'settle' mean? What do they seem ready to do there just to be in a job? How does that reduce them as human beings? Cathay was the name for the region of China and Japan when it was thought to be the richest place in the world and everyone wanted to get at its riches. Why are 'Cathay shores' (l 41) mentioned in connection with these emigrants?

4 Is the speaker in the poem pitying the 'them' or mocking them? Say why you come to your opinion.

Soil p109

1 Mangolds and swedes are not grown in the West Indies. What do you take 'plying mechanically' (l 6) to mean? 'This is his world' (l 7). What is the this that is his world? What accident sometimes happens?

2 What is the speaker in the poem implying by saying 'the hedge defines the mind's limits' (ll 7-8)? Why does the speaker say 'The soil is all' (l 11)? Is the speaker suggesting that the 'he' should have something else? Is the speaker regarding the 'he' with admiration or sorrow? Give a reason for your view.

3 Is there anything similar between this poem and The Earth is Brown (p89)?

A Black Man Talks of Reaping p110

1 What do you think the 'I' means by 'I have sown' (l 1)? Why had he 'planted deep' (l 2)? How does he give an idea of the amount of sowing he did in his lifetime?

2 What do you gather from lines 7-8 about the rewards he received for his labour? Who are gathering the fruits of his toil? To whom do you think he is referring as 'my brother's sons' (l 10)?

3 How do you interpret 'my children glean in fields they have not sown' (ll 11-12)? What do you imagine are the 'bitter fruit' (l 12)?

4 The whole poem is a sustained *metaphor* with several metaphors within it. What is the metaphor in 'wind or fowl would take the grain away' (l 3); 'what the hand can hold at once' (l 8); 'what the orchard yields' (l 9)? How would you describe the tone of voice in it? Why?

Maljo's Political Party p110

1 These lines are from a poem of more than 8000 lines called
  Omeros which tells about the people of St. Lucia, comparing some
  of them to people in a poem about 2000 years old called *The
  Odyssey* by the Greek poet, Homer. Who are the people mentioned
  in this excerpt from *Omeros*?

2 'Philoctete peered at each candidate' (ll 3-4). What were they
  candidates for? Who do you think was 'screaming for Workers'
  Rights' (l 2)? What did Philoctete ask Maljo in the rumshop?
  Whom did Maljo mean by 'them two men' (l 10)?

3 Why did Maljo 'pay his deposit' and 'rent Hector's transport' (l 11)?
  What was the megaphone for? Where did Maljo hold the first
  meeting of his political campaign? Who were the people who
  became his followers?

4 In the island's superstitions the word 'maljo' is the name given to
  bad luck that someone is supposed to have wished on you out of
  envy. Do you think that has any connection with the name of the
  character in the story? How does it make him appear, dignified or
  unfortunate? How does his behaviour with the megaphone make
  him look, capable or untaught? Would you admire him or laugh at
  him? Why?

5 How do you interpret 'A new age would begin' (l 27)? Charter
  yachts brought wealthy tourists to the island. Why, do you imagine,
  did Maljo still have 'barefoot followers'
  (l 19)? Why do you suppose his party's sign or symbol was 'a
  broken chain dangling from a black hand' (l 33)? Who do you think
  he meant by 'the oppressor' (l 34)? What do you understand about
  Maljo from lines 43-49? Would you say he was trying to do a good
  thing or not? Why?

6 The poet portrays the candidate who had the poor in mind as being
  unable to achieve effective leadership. What do you suppose was
  the poet's intention in doing that? In what way is the excerpt
  condemning how the poor are treated?

Sometimes In The Middle of The Story p112

1 The Middle Passage, as you should know, was the name given to
  the route the slave ships took when bringing Africans to be slaves in
  the West Indies and the American colonies. Many Africans who

became too ill on the voyage were thrown overboard. Toussaint L'Ouverture was the son of a slave in Haiti. He was literate, and in 1801 led the slaves to revolt against the French who owned them. It was the only successful slave revolt in history and it set Haiti free. Toussaint's real name was Toussaint Breda but he came to be called L'Ouverture, which means gap or opening, because his strategy as a general was to get his troops to make gaps in the French lines of defence. In the poem, who said they heard Toussaint passing?

2   Why according to the poem, did the story-teller hesitate? What, in the poem did the old people think of Toussaint as doing? What else were they reminded of? With whom did they imagine Toussaint had a secret meeting? Where? Who are 'those who never completed the journey' (l 19)? Who were those 'below deck' (l 20)? What do lines 20-26 (the muffled . . . closing over) describe?

3   Whose souls are said to 'shuttle still the forest paths of the ocean' (l 26)? 'connecting us still' (l 27). Connecting whom? In what way could they be 'connecting'? What do you imagine 'the tireless messengers' (l 26) are messengers of? What do you suppose is the 'power' 'rising from the sea' (l 30)? Who are called 'princes' (l 29)? Why? Could every captured African be a prince? Do you detect sentimentality in that or anywhere else in the poem?

4   The poem begins as if someone is telling ghost stories to children. What would you say is the story-telling that the poem suggests should take place? The poet did not use strictly correct, grammatical English but the voice of a West Indian in everyday conversation. Why do you think he did that? Would you say that that increases your pleasure or not? Give a reason for your answer.

Tom p113

1   'Here old Tom lived' (l 17). How large was the place? Why is it called a 'cracked limestone oblong' (l 45)? What signs of age does it now show? How does the yard show signs of neglect? What would you take 'time's long attack' (ll 28-29) to mean?

2   What new buildings have been built in the village? How would you interpret 'But the tide creeps in: today's insistence laps the loneliness of this resisting cabin' (ll 38-40)?

3   What do you imagine from 'No one knows Tom now' (ll 50-51) and 'Slave's days are past, forgotten' (ll 52-53)? Was Tom a slave? What

do you think the poet intends a reader to understand from the last
six lines (ll 53-58)? What do you imagine from 'dream' (l 53), 'all
lost' (l 55), and 'hurt' (l 57)? How would you connect 'banged like a
fist' (l 20) with lines 53-58?

Hill Houses p115

1 'Hill houses' are often rich people's houses outside a town. Is that
   the case in this poem? What makes you say so?
2 What dangers do they face? What would happen if they came true?
3 Which images do you find most vivid and full of feeling?
4 What do the last six lines tell you about the people? What feeling
   do they bring to you?

In my Fourteenth Year p117

1 This excerpt comes from a book-length poem called *Another Life* in
   which the poet tells of his early life in St. Lucia. What connection do
   you see in these lines between 'I lost my self' (l 2), not 'myself', and
   'I dissolved into a trance' (l 8)?
2 Where was the 'I' in the poem? When was he there? Whose houses
   were nearby? Hovels are like huts and scrim is a thin transparent
   cloth. Why do you suppose those things are mentioned?
3 'I was seized by a pity' (l 9). Why? What do you imagine is meant
   by 'I began to weep, inwardly, without tears' (ll 13-14)? What
   seemed to have been the 'everything' (l 16) wept for? What do you
   think could cause a person to just weep 'for nothing' (l 16)?
4 How are the poor being regarded when these phrases are said:
   'their lights still shine' (l 22) and 'lamp still slowly says its
   prayer' (l 23)? Why are 'chains' mentioned? Are we to be
   reminded of something in history by 'in that ship of night locked
   in together' (l 26)? What do you think the 'something' in the last
   line could be?

To the Madwoman in my Yard p118

1 In Kingston, Jamaica, the Dungle (l 15) is a shanty area and
   Barbican (l 14) is a well-to-do area. Where was the person called
   'Lady' throwing rocks? What do you learn about her from 'So you
   choose out of doors' (ll 21-22)? What do lines 23-24 tell you about
   her behaviour? What reasons does she give for it? In lines 17-21

what does the other person in the poem, the speaker, imagine as the kind of events in the life of the 'Lady'?

2 What does 'when I'm gardening' (l 5) tell you about the life of the speaker in the poem? Try to explain 'Here I am . . . Society' (ll 10-11). How do you interpret line 13? In what way did the 'Lady' bring it 'right in' (l 12)? How do you imagine the speaker was trying hard 'With Society' (l 11)? In 'trying to escape' (l 13), what do you think the speaker had to do? A 'maelstrom' (l 15) means a confusing state of affairs. How then would you interpret 'a Barbican gate . . . maelstrom' (ll 14-15)? Why should the speaker be in a maelstrom?

3 What do you think the speaker means by 'Life Equals Control' (l 25)? How would you interpret 'I wear my madness in' (l 27)? Is there a connection between that and 'With Society' (l 11) and 'maelstrom' (l 15)? Why would the speaker refer to her life as 'my madness'? How true do you think is the speaker's claim 'you don't move me one blast' (l 25)? What do you think the speaker feels about the 'Lady'? What problem of conscience does the speaker seem to have?

4 Behind the speaker's angry words there is something else in the *tone* of voice. What would you say it is? What part do you see *irony* playing in the poem?

A Storm Passes p119

1 These lines come from *Omeros*. Read about it in the questions on *Maljo's Political Party* (p110). Why were the valleys 'devastated' (l 1)? What meaning do you give to each of these: a) 'roads that were rivers' (l 3); b) 'the slaughter of the year's banana crop' (l 3-4); c) 'made islands of villages' (l 9); d) 'shouldered culverts aside' (10); e) 'tossed up the salad of trees' (l 24)?

2 Castanets are small pieces of wood held between the fingers and clicked together to keep time. Apart from the meaning of the words, what kind of *sound* do you hear in a) 'contractors in white helmets and slickers heard the castanets' (ll 25-26); b) 'the tunnels of brown water roaring in the mangroves' (ll 13-14)? Is this *onomatopoeia*?

3 The poet shows the richness of his imagination when he gives us fresh, telling, remarkable metaphors. Point to the ones in these lines that you consider most memorable.

Ode to Brother Joe
Anthony McNeill   Jamaica

Nothing can soak
Brother Joe's tough sermon,
his head swollen
with certainties.

5   When he lights up a s'liff[1]
you can't stop him,
and the door to God, usually shut,
gives in a rainbow gust.

Then it's time for the pipe,
10 which is filled with its water base
and handed to him for his blessing.
He bends over the stem,
goes into the long grace,
and the drums start,

15 *the drums start*
Haile Selassie I
Jah Rastafari,
And the room fills with the power
and beauty of blackness,
20 a furnace of optimism.[2]

But the law thinks different.
This evening the Babylon[3] catch
Brother Joe in his act of praise
and carted him off to the workhouse.[4]

25 Who'll save Brother Joe? Haile
Selassie is far away
and couldn't care less,
and the promised ship

is a million light years
30 from Freeport.

But the drums in the tenement house
are sadder than usual tonight,

and the brothers suck hard
at their s'liffs and pipes:
35 Before the night's over,
Brother joe has become a martyr;

But still in jail;
And only his woman
who appreciates his *humanness* more
40 will deny herself of the weed⁵ tonight
to hire a lawyer
and put up a real fight.

Meantine, in the musty cell,
Joe invokes, almost from habit,
45 the magic words:
Haile Selassie I
Jah Rastafari,
But the door is real and remains shut.

¹ *s'liff* – spliff, marijuana cigarette
² *optimism* – hope, positive attitudes
³ *Babylon* – police
⁴ *workhouse* – prison
⁵ *weed* – ganja, marijuana

The James Bond Movie
May Swenson   *USA*

The popcorn is greasy, and I forgot to bring a Kleenex.
A pill that's a bomb inside the stomach of a man inside

The Embassy blows up. Eructations¹ of flame, luxurious
cauliflowers giganticize into motion. The entire 29-ft.

5 screen is orange, is crackling flesh and brick bursting,
blackening, smithereened. I unwrap a Dentyne and, while

jouncing my teeth in rubber tongue-smarting clove, try
with the 2-inch-wide paper to blot butter off my fingers.

a bubble-bath, room-sized, in which 14 girls, delectable[2]
10 and sexless, twist-topped Creamy Freezes[3] (their blonde,

red, brown, pinkish, lavender or silver wiglets all
screwed that high, and varnished), scrub-tickle a lone

male, whose chest has just the right amount and distrib-
tion of curly hair. He's nervously pretending to defend

15 his modesty. His crotch, below the waterline, is also
below the frame – but unsubmerged all 28 slick foamy boobs.

Their makeup fails to let the girls look naked. Caterpil-
lar lashes, black and thick, lush lips glossed pink like

the gum I pop and chew, contact lenses on the eyes that are
20 mostly blue, they're nose-perfet replicas[4] of each other.
I've got most of the grease off and onto this little square
of paper. I'm folding it now, making creases with my nails.

[1] *eructations* – belches, burps, eruptions
[2] *delectable* – delightful, pleasant
[3] *Creamy Freezes* – ice cream cones
[4] *replicas* – copies

Child with a Dead Animal
Judith Wright   *Australia*

The thing you saw set your eyes running tears
faster than words could tell;
the creature changed to thing, kindness to dread,
the warm shape chilled, forsaken, left for dead –
5   these crowded up to blind your eyes; these fell,

and fell till it seemed you'd wash away with tears
the glimpse you'd had of death
and clear it from your heart. It was not true.
The sight you saw had found its home in you.
10 It breathed now in your breath,

crouched in your glance. From it those gasping tears
fell, and will always fall.
They mark you Man, whose very earth is made
of light's encounter with its answering shade.
15 Take then this bread, this wine; be part of all.

Cold Beds
David Sweetman   *England*

Thirty years she had waited for disaster
and when they told her he had drowned
she nodded. Like things seen in Holy prints

5 there had been signs: the greengrocer
piling bound asparagus as if to burn a saint
made her cross herself quickly.

And when she took flowers for Bob
a dead gull lay on the boy's grave,
plump and grey as the shell that killed him.
10

So now the father's gone, after thirty years
on a bed too big for one she sees it all:
the sails becalmed at the window,

her Madonna[1] for a prow, the moonlight
15 that gives their walnut cupboard the pattern
of waves closing over his head.

[1] *Madonna* – figure of the Virgin Mary

Airy Hall's Dark Age
Fred D'Aguiar   *Guyana*

Someone's, 'The child is a cross,
He has bad blood through and through,'
Is picked up and amplified[1] across fields.

These vocals stick somewhere in the acres
5 This town covers, against a gale
On its way to tearing up islands.
A child doing the things
Children do: dly, brash,[2] fidgety,
Becomes aligned[3] with the devil.

10 All that remains is for one among us
To fetch the pint-sized stake[4]
Dressed in razor-grass and bramble.

No sooner the child is ambushed,
An empty paddy-bag he raced in
15 Swooped over his head and tied,

Rough-shod above waist level,
A lasso from a hand he looked up to
And he is beyond us all.

[1] *amplified* – made louder
[2] *brash* – bold, forward, rude
[3] *aligned* – said to be linked with
[4] *stake* – wooden pole to which people said to be witches were tied and burned

A Stone's Throw
Elma Mitchell   *Scotland*

We shouted out
'We've got her' Here she is!
It's her all right'.
We caught her.
5 There she was –

A decent-looking woman, you'd have said,
(They often are)
Beautiful, but dead scared,
Tousled¹ we roughed her up
10 A little, nothing much
And not the first time
By any means
She'd felt men's hands
Over her body –
15 But ours were virtuous,
Of course.

And if our fingers bruised
Her shuddering skin,
These were love-bites, compared
20 To the hail of kisses of stone,
The last assault
And battery, frigid rape,
To come
Of right.
25 For justice must be done
Specially when
It tastes so good.

And then – this guru,
Peacher. God-merchant, God-knows-what-
30 Spoilt the whole thing
Speaking to her
(Should never speak to them)
Squatting on the ground – her level,
Writing in the dust
35 Something we couldn't read.

And saw in her
Something we couldn't see,
At least until
He turned his eyes on us,
40 Her eyes on us,
Our eyes upon ourselves.

We walked away
Still holding stones
That we may throw
45 Another day
Given the urge.

Christ Climbed Down
Lawrence Ferlinghetti   *USA*

Christ climbed down
from His bare tree
this year
and ran away to where
5 there were no rootless Christmas trees
hung with candycanes and breakable stars

Christ climbed down
from His bare tree
this year
10 and ran away to where

there were no gilded Christmas trees
and no tinsel Christmas trees
and no tinfoil Christmas trees
and no pink plastic Christmas trees
15 and no gold Christmas trees
and no black Christmas trees
and no powder blue Christmas trees
hung with electric candles
and encircled by tin electric trains
20 and clever cornball¹ relatives
Christ climbed down
from His bare tree
this year
and ran away to where
25 no intrepid² Bible salesmen

covered the territory
in two-tone cadillacs
and where no Sears Roebuck creches[3]
complete with plastic babe in manger
30   arrived by parcel post
the babe by special delivery
and where no televised Wise Men
praised the Lord Calvert Whiskey

Christ climbed down
35   from His bare tree
this year
and ran away to where
no fat handshaking stranger
in a red flannel suit
40   and a fake white beard
went around passing himself off
as some sort of North Pole saint
crossing the desert to Bethlehem
Pennsylvania
45   in a Volkswagon sled
drawn by rollicking Adirondack[4] reindeer
with German names
and bearing sacks of Humble Gifts
from Saks Fifth Avenue
50   for everybody's imagined Christ child

Christ climbed down
from His bare tree
this year
and ran away to where
55   no Bing Crosby carollers
groaned of a tight Christmas
and where no Radio City[5] angels
iceskated wingless
thru a winter wonderland
60   into a jinglebell heaven
daily at 8:30
with Midnight Mass matinees

Christ climbed down
from His bare tree
65 this year
and softly stole away into
some annymous Mary's womb again
where in the darkest night
of everybody's anonymous soul
70 He awaits again
an unimaginable
and impossibly
Immaculate Reconception
the very craziest
75 of Second Comings

¹ *cornball* – dull, stale, corny
² *intrepid* – adventurous, brave
³ *creches* – representations of the scene of the birth of Christ, the Nativity scene
⁴ *Adirondack* – a mountainous part of the US
⁵ *Radio City* – place in New York for musical shows

Funeral Rites I
Seamus Heaney   *Ireland*

I shouldered a kind of manhood
stepping in to lift the coffins
of dead relations.
They had been laid out

5 in tainted rooms,
their eyelids glistening,
their dough-white hands
shackled in rosary beads.

Their puffed knuckles
10 had unwrinkled, the nails
were darkened, the wrists
obediently sloped.

The dulse-brown shroud,
the quilted-satin cribs:
15   I knelt courteously
admiring it all

as wax melted down
and veined the candles,
the flames hovering
20   to the women hovering

behind me.
And always, in a corner,
the coffin lid,
its nail-heads dressed

25   with little gleaming crosses.
Dear soapstone[1] masks,
kissing their igloo brows
had to suffice

before the nails were sunk
30   and the black glacier[2]
of each funeral pushed away.

[1] *soapstone* – a soft white stone or powder, like talc
[2] *glacier* – mass of flowing ice

Airy Hall's Exits
Fred D'Aguiar   *Guyana*

Salt over the shoulder
Or a trip curtailed,
On account of the black cat
That crossed your path.

5   Last rites for the sick
In a house a crow
Overflew or preened itself on
And cawed, cawed, cawed.[1]

A black dress, the gift
10 From a relative you've never seen,
For the funeral of a friend
You never imagined could die.

The dream you fall in,
Waking seconds before you land,
15 Your heart backfiring; the dream
You one day fail to wake from.

[1] *cawed* – made crow sounds

Tabiz

*'Long time ago they used to say
How jumbie used to walk the road'*
Anson Gonzales   *Trinidad and Tobago*

this poem is to cut maljo
is to save you from the blight
of overloving eyes that conceal hate
from over-generous eyes that subsume[1]
5 the bitter bile of envy
from judas-friendly eyes that shut
bestowing the betraying kiss

like a blue bottle on a stick
it will ward off whatsoever evil
10 may try to wither the bounty
of your blooming life's garden

keep it there and no beetle
no bug no worm no fly no snake
will invade and your life
15 will be a blossoming eden

then you'll sing your happy songs
in the peaceful harmony you wish
and all your joys will be unsullied[2]

or wear it like a mystic amulet[3]
20 or a ringlet of blue-black beads
or yet like a blessed ankh[4]
and fell your confidence rise
as you scale the unsurmountable
wear it and you'll climb your everests[5]
25 as easily as your el tucuches[6]
or make of it a magic circle
to protect and comfort you
step into it as my friend's mother once
IN HOC VINCIT[7] and with signs
30 defied her enemies
and the evil ones
we'll chant the aves halleluias
the hosannas the alaikums and oms[8]
we'll bring the greater glory
35 to your assistance and you will
rise and soar

or make it a stole of blue
draping your possessed shoulders
making all your ancestral contacts
40 give you great strength

encircled by the indigoed[9] words
you will bravely step through
legs of phantoms
put salt on soucouyant[10] skins
45 make doens[11] disappear
and you'll dance in life's moonlight
safe from all harm

[1] *subsume* – take in, include
[2] *unsullied* – pure, clean
[3] *amulet* – good look around
[4] *ankh* – an ancient Egyptian symbol of life
[5] *Everest* – highest point in the world
[6] *El Tucuches* – highest point in Trinidad
[7] *IN HOC VINCIT* – Latin for 'won a victory in this place'
[8] *the hosannas the alaikums and oms* – chants of praise
[9] *indigoed* – coloured blue
[10] *soucouyant* – person believed to shed skin at night, old higues
[11] *doens* – devils of the forest

A City's Death by Fire
Derek Walcott   *St Lucia*

After that hot gospeller had levelled all but the churched sky,
I wrote the tale by tallow[1] of a city's death by fire;
Under a candle's eye, that smoked in tears, I
Wanted to tell, in more than wax, of faiths that were snapped
    like wire.
5 All day I walked abroad among the rubbled[2] tales,
Shocked at each wall that stood on the street like a liar;
Loud was the bird-rocked sky, and all the clouds were bales
Torn open by looting, and white, in spite of the fire.
By the smoking sea, where Christ walked, I asked why
10 Should a man wax tears, when his wooden world fails?
In town, leaves were paper, but the hills were a flock of faiths;
To a boy who walked all day, each leaf was a green breath
Rebuilding a love I thought was dead as nails,
Blessing the death and the baptism by fire.

[1] *tallow* – candle
[2] *rubbled* – fallen into fragments of stone, pieces

Discussion and Activities

Ode to Brother Joe p128

1 Who do you suppose Brother Joe to be? What clues do you use in the poem to tell you? What is the *weed* (l 40)?

2 What happened to Brother Joe? Why?

3 What would you say is the full meaning of these lines: 2-4; 28-30; 35-36?

4 Which of these best describe the poet's mood and tone of voice? a) scorn and contempt; b) deep anger and ridicule; c) mild grief, compassion and anger; d) humour and laughter; e) bitterness and hatred. Choose phrases and lines which you consider important to this question.

The James Bond Movie p129

1 While watching the movie the speaker eats popcorn and then has a problem. What does he/she do about it? Why would you infer the speaker is female? If you've ever seen a James Bond movie you would have seen something like what is described in lines 2-6. Why do you suppose such movies have scenes like that all the time? What scene follows the blowing up of the Embassy? What do you take 'scrub-tickle' (l 12) to mean?

2 What criticisms are suggested about the girls in lines 10-12? What opinion is the speaker expressing about films like that when she observes 'they're nose-perfect replicas of each other' (l 20)?

3 Which stereotyped movie image is the speaker mocking when she says 'a lone male whose chest has the right amount and distribution of curly hair' (ll 12-14)? Could that also be a criticism of women who are impressed by men they call 'macho' and 'he-men'? What does 'modesty' (l 15) mean? How does the man behave while the girls scrub-tickle him? Who is amused when he pretends? Why do you suppose he is not exposed in the film but the girls are? What about them is being exploited to provide entertainment and money for others? Anger often makes a woman use her nails. Is the 'I' in the poem 'making creases with her nails' (l 22) merely to fold the paper or out of anger about something? If it is anger, anger about what?

4 In which lines does the poet use sensational, exaggerated language to suit the sensational, exaggerated matter on the screen? What tone of voice do you hear from the words of the 'I' in the poem? Where do you detect strong sarcasm? What would you say is the attitude of the 'I' to a) films like that, and b) the use of women's bodies in films and photographs to entertain viewers? Defend your opinion.

Child with a Dead Animal p130

1 'The sight you saw had found its home in you' (l 9). What sight? In what way had it found a home? In what other poems have you met a similar idea expressed?
2 'They mark you Man' (l 13). What does the writer mean by this statement and the rest of the poem?

Cold Beds p131

1 'she nodded' (l 3). When? What meaning do you give to 'Thirty years she had waited for disaster' (l 1)? Does 'waited for' mean 'expected'? Which signs did she believe in?
2 Why is the bed 'too big for one' (l 11)? 'she sees it all' (l 11). What does 'sees' mean? Which sails were 'becalmed at the window' (l 12)? Why did the moonlight on the cupboard make her see waves? Why is the poem called *Cold Beds*?

Airy Hall's Dark Age p132

1 What is 'picked up and amplified' (l 3)? How is the child described in lines 7-8? How do you interpret line 9? What is the importance of 'All that remains' (l 10)? Remains after what?
2 Long ago persons found guilty of something against what was considered sacred were burned at the stake. More recently, black people in the USA were lynched: taken by mobs and hanged if they were suspected of what was regarded as a crime. What meaning would you give to lines 10-11? Why 'pint-sized' (l 11)? What is being described in lines 14-18? Is the child really ambushed and lynched?
3 Which stanza would you say tells what made the poet write the poem? How do you know how he feels about 'these vocals' (14)? Is the speaker in the poem speaking with a stern, a sorrowful, or a sarcastic voice? What makes you sense his attitude?

A Stone's Throw p132

1 In some cultures in the past, and in some still, adulteresses and prostitutes were stoned to death. In the Christian bible, in the book of St John, a story is told of an adulteress who was held and brought to Jesus. He was asked why she should not be stoned to death, according to the law of Moses. He replied, 'Let him that is without sin cast the first stone.' He then stooped down and wrote with his finger in the dust and the Pharisees slinked off, ashamed. He spoke to the woman and said, 'Go, and sin no more.' With regard to the woman in the poem, when do you imagine 'fingers bruised her shuddering skin' (ll 17-18)? Whose fingers? Who do you think shouted 'We've got her' (l 12)? Why, do you suppose, 'She'd felt men's hands/Over her body' (ll 13-14)? How was she to get 'kisses of stone' (l 20)? Why?

2 Who would you say is the narrator in the poem? Who do you think is referred to as 'this guru, Preacher' (l 19)? Why does the narrator say 'Spoilt the whole thing' (l 30)? What happened? How would you interpret 'And saw in her Something we couldn't see' (ll 36-37)? What do you take 'Our eyes upon ourselves' (l 41) to mean?

3 Would you agree that the bible story is more vivid to you as told in this poem? Try to explain why you agree or disagree. How, would you say, did the poet make the message or lesson from the bible have more present-day relevance and impact? What points of comparison can you find between this poem and *Christ Climbed Down* (p.134)?

Christ Climbed Down p134

1 Why, would you say, does the speaker mention things which are 'gilded' (l 11), of 'tinsel' and 'tinfoil', 'pink plastic', and so on? Do any of these worthless things used at Christmas make people follow what Christ said about loving one another? Why do you think the speaker said that Christ ran where no 'Bible salesman' (l 25), mass produced Navitity 'creches' (l 28), and Christmas TV advertisements for 'Lord Calvert Whiskey' (l 33) were? What do you sense the speaker's attitude to be to all that with respect to the real message of Christ?

2 Who is referred to 'in a red flannel suit and a fake white beard' (ll 39-40)? Why do you think the speaker said that Christ ran away

from where that person was? Why do you suppose the speaker said Christ avoided 'Bing Crosby carollers', *'Winter Wonderland'* and *'Jingle Bells'*? What is the speaker suggesting about people who pay attention to them? What else does the speaker say Christ avoided?

3 What do you suppose is 'His bare tree' (l 2)? How significant is the symbol of that tree to Christians? What kind of message would Christ be sending if the tree were vacated? What is the poem suggesting that Christ is protesting about? Why do you suppose the speaker said that Christ went back to a womb to wait to be able to come again? What do you think the speaker is saying indirectly about Christians and Christianity? In your view, then, what is the poem really concerned about? Would you agree with the view that Christ in the poem is a symbol for a way of life and that it is the way of life that ran away? Try to give a reasoned explanation for agreeing or disagreeing.

4 Is the speaker being just amusing or disrespectful or sarcastic when he/she says 'clever cornball relative' (l 20); 'two-tone cadillacs' (l 27); 'complete with plastic babe' (l 29); 'televised Wise Men' (l 32); 'fat handshaking stranger' (l 38); 'passing himself off' (l 41); 'some sort of North Pole saint' (l 42)? Find other phrases in which the same tone of voice comes through. Do you think the speaker weakens his/her case and turns you against what he/she is saying by being so satirical about things that people do and like? Do you find any similarity between this poem and *A Stone's Throw* (p132)?

Funeral Rites I p136

1 Roman Catholics use a string of beads, called a rosary. Whose hands were 'shackled in rosary beads' (l 8)? How do you know they did not have dark skins? Where were they? Quote phrases put into the poem to give pictures or imagery of the 'dead relations' (l 3). What do you imagine to be 'Dear soapstone masks' (l 26)?

2 What do you think is described as 'quilted satin cribs' (l 14)? How did the melting candle appear? What was always in the corner of the room? Always when? An igloo is a dome of ice. Why were their foreheads called 'igloo brows' (l 27)? How do you interpret lines 27-29? Which nails were sunk? Where? Why do you suppose the funeral is described as a 'black glacier' (l 30)?

3 'I shouldered a kind of manhood' (l 1). Was the 'I' a man? Do you see any connection between his age and 'I knelt courteously admiring it all' (ll 15-16)? Would you say the poet wrote this poem merely to describe funerals he was involved in, or for some other reason? What makes you say so?

4 It is possible that the melting candle (ll 17-18) could be a symbol of something else in those circumstances. Do you think it is? Could the 'nails' have certain associations and connotations in such an atmosphere? What might they be? Or could the nails also be a symbol? If so, of what?

Airy Hall's Exits p137

1 The poem tells of certain superstitious beliefs. Which one is referred to in the first stanza? In the second stanza? The third stanza? The fourth?

2 The poet has called a certain place in Guyana 'Airy Hall'. Why do you suppose the poem is named *Airy Hall's Exits*? Which exits are the stuff of the poem?

Tabiz p138

1 In the local superstitious 'maljo' (l 1) means bad luck a person has all the time because of someone's envy and obeh, (witchcraft). 'Blight' (l 2) means continuing bad luck. For whom, do you suppose, was the poem made?

2 Local superstitious persons believe that something blue should be worn as a charm or amulet against 'maljo'. Explain lines 8-11. Why 'blue-black beads' (l 20)? Why 'a stole of blue' (l 37)? 'Indigoed words' (l 41)? What is the 'it' the 'I' refers to in 'wear it' (l 19)? In 'make of it' (l 26)? In 'step into it' (l 28)? In 'make it' (l 37)?

3 A 'soucouyant' (l 44) in the local superstitions is supposed to be a woman who sheds her skin at night and flies to suck the blood of sleeping victims – a kind of flying Dracula. In Guyana the term 'old higue' is used. In the superstitious myths of the place 'douens' (l 45) are demons that live in the forests. In your own words say which evils the 'you' is warned against in lines 3-7, 12-14, 43-45.

4 The 'I' connects certain benefits with the gift of the poem. They are referred to in different places in the poem. Which lines mention them?

5 In the phrase 'bitter bile' (l 5) alliteration occurs. Is there any alliteration in lines 7, 8, 20, 34, 44, 45?

A City's Death by Fire p140

1 The city of the poem is the town of Castries in St Lucia which was destroyed by fire in 1948 when the poet was 18 years old. From the poem what do you see of the destruction? Which lines and phrases bring the scene most vividly to you?

2 In line 4 what does the poet say he wanted to do? What 'faiths' do you suppose he refers to?

3 What question did he ask in line 10? What do you judge to be the importance of the phrase 'his wooden world fails' on understanding the theme of the poem?

4 What connection can you see, if any, between 'faiths that were snapped' (l 4), 'wooden world fails' (l 10), 'a flock of faiths' (l 11) and 'the baptism by fire' (l 14)?

Rampanalgas
Wayne Brown   *Trinidad and Tobago*

Rust stiffens the louvres, but we hook
them open a crack for one more look
at the ocean. Overhead, palm trees like hefted[1] squid[2]
lean seaward, trailing their tentacles,
5   useless in air.

We are born here
once only, then like the octopus left
to darken white seas, ink rising through foam,
to print near this beach hut the one word, Home.

10   Now, years later, I watch this shack,
the heart's first effort, rusting shut,
and turn from the glass. At my back
the ocean tries
the first steps up to this house, and falls back.

[1] *hefted* – lifted
[2] *squid* – a creature like an octopus

Dry Season Nights
Alan Hollinghurst   *England*

Dry season nights you wake at one or two
to hear dead leaves skip crabwise on the path,
the palm-fronds gust and rattle
like water splashing in an unstopped sink . . .
5   A dried-out spider in its ball of thread
is blown along the floor; stamped postcards
fan themselves upon the sill, and you remember
other friendships gone like water from a saucer.

Slick, shuffling demons of the carnival,
10   the Jab-Jab[1] boys have bodies black with oil;

they grab you if you do not give them coins.
Half-scared, you gave too much, and then regretted,
not giving but not having been abused
by devils whose worst weapon is a hug
15 (such liquid blackness, blackness that comes off,
daubed handprints on those tropic cottons . . .)

Pink by sunset, from the yellow lawn
you watch the pink and yellow afterglow.
You shower carefully from a dribbling pipe
10 and light a slowly smoking insect coil.
The breeze sifts through the open louvres
and levitates[2] the single sheet;
the wind slams from the hill above
and sits down with a sigh on the edge of the bed.

[1] *lab-lab* – a kind of masquerader in Trinidad's carnival
[2] *levitates* – lifts

At Home the Green Remains
John Figueroa   *Jamaica*

In England now I hear the window shake
And see beyond its astigmatic[1] pane
Against black limbs Autumn's yellow stain
Splashed about tree-tops and wet beneath the rake.
5 New England's hills are flattened as crimson-lake
And purple columns, all that now remain
Of trees, stand forward as hillocks do in rain,
And up the hillside ruined temples make.

At home the green remains: the palm throws back
10 Its head and breathes above the still blue sea,
The separate hills are lost in common blue
Only the splendid poinsettias, true
And crimson like the northern ivy, tack,
But late, the yearly notice to a tree.

[1] *astigmatic* – with unclear, twisted vision
[2] *hillocks* – low hills

Welsh Landscape

R.S. Thomas   *Wales*

To live in Wales is to be conscious
At dusk of the spilled blood
That went to the making of the wild sky,
Dyeing the immaculate rivers
5 In all their courses.
It is to be aware,
Above the noisy tractor
And hum of the machine
Of strife in the strung woods,
10 Vibrant with sped arrows.
You cannot live in the present,
At least not in Wales:
There is the language for instance,
The soft consonants
15 Strange to the ear.
There are cries in the dark at night
As owls answer the moon,
And thick ambush[1] of shadows,
Hushed at the fields' cornets.
20 There is no present in Wales,
And no future;
There is only the past,
Brittle[2] with relics[3];
Wind-bitten towers and castles
25 With sham ghosts;
Mouldering quarries and mines;
And an impotent[4] people,
Sick with inbreeding.
Worrying the carcase[5] of an old song.

[1] *ambush* – trap, taking by surprise
[2] *brittle* – easily broken
[3] *relics* – remaining, tokens of rememberance
[4] *impotent* – powerless
[5] *carcase* – dead body

Islands

Edward Brathwaite *Barbados*

So looking through a map
of the islands, you see
rocks, history's hot
lies, rot-
5 ting hills, cannon
wheels, the sun's
slums: if you hate
us. Jewels,
if there is delight
10 in your eyes.
The light
shimmers on water,
the cunning
coral keeps it
15 blue.

Looking through a map
of the Antilles, you see how time
has trapped
its humble servants here. De-
20 scendants of the slave do not
lie in the lap
of the more fortunate
gods. The rat
in the warehouse is as much king
25 as the sugar he plunders.
But if your eyes
are kinder, you will observe
butterflies
how they fly higher
30 and higher before their hope dries
with endeavour
and they fall among flies.

Looking through a map
of the islands, you see
35 that history teaches
that when hope
splinters, when the pieces
of broken glass lie
in the sunlight,
40 when only lust rules
the night, when the dust
is not swept out
of the houses,
when men make noises
45 louder than the sea's
voices; then the rope
will never unravel
its knots, the branding
iron's travelling flame that teaches
50 us pain, will never be
extinguished. The islands' jewels:
Saba, Barbuda, dry flat-
tened Antigua, will remain rocks,
dots, in the sky-blue frame
55 of the map.

There is a Mystic Splendour
Raymond Barrow   *Belize*

There is a mystic[1] splendour that one feels
Walking this shore in the half-light of dawn,
Placing one's footprints on the sands where keels
Of ancient vessels must have beached and drawn.

5 For there are tales that speak of glorious days
When martial[2] shouting rang within our Bay,
And cannons thundered, and black battle haze
Clouded this sickle[3] isle with dark affray.[4]

Those were the times when privateers fled
10 The predatory⁵ Brethren of the Coast;
Pirates and buccaneers – all these are dead,
And all their lordly sway seems but a ghost.

But even now the surf's loud thunder brings
Sound strangely clear – like battle cries of old;
15 And palm trees murmur of deep-sunken things,
Of buried treasure chests . . . and Morgan's gold . . .

¹ *mystic* – spiritual
² *martial* – military
³ *sickle* – curved
⁴ *affray* – rioting, fighting
⁵ *predatory* – looking for others to prey on

Leaving Home (from *Another Life*)
Derek Walcott   *St Lucia*

One dawn the sky was warm pink thinning to no colour.
In it, above the Morne¹, the last star shone
measuring the island with its callipers.²
As usual, everywhere, the sinuations³ of cockcrow,
5   a leisured, rusting, rising and falling,
echoed the mountain line. The day creaked
wearily open. A wash of meagre blue entered the sky.
The final star diminished and withdrew.
Day pivoted⁴ on a sea-gull's screeching hinge.
10 And the year closed. The allamandas fell,
medalling the shoulders of the last visitor.
At the airport, I looked towards the beach.
The sand had seen battalions come and go,
the vines had written their memorials,
15 all of that cannonfire taken up by cloud.
Nothing had altered the teal or mallard's route,
all that salt blood thinned out in the salt surf.
I shook Gregorias's hand. Dead almond leaf.
There was no history. No memory.
20 Rocks haunted by sea-birds, that was all.

The house would survive, my brother would survive,
and yet how arrogant, how cruel
to think the island and Anna would survive
(since they were one), inviolate[6], under
25 their sacred and inverted bell of glass,
and that I was incapable of betrayal,
to imagine their lives revolving round my future,
to accept as natural their selfless surrender.
The three faces I had most dearly loved
30 that year, among the blurred faces in the crowd,
Gregorias laughing, "Jamaica just up the road, man,
just up the road." Harry hustling. Anna had not moved.
I watched the island narrowing, the fine
writing of foam around the precipices, then
35 the roads as small and casual as twine
thrown on its mountains, I watched till the plane
turned to the final north and turned above
the open channel with the grey sea between
the fishermen's islets until all that I love
40 folded in cloud. I watched the shallow green
breaking in places where there would be reef,
the silver glinting on the fuselage[7], each mile
tightening us and all fidelity[8] strained
till space would snap it. Then, after a while
45 I thought of nothing, nothing I prayed, would change.
When we set down at Seawell it had rained.

[1] *Morne* – a hill in Castries, St. Lucia
[2] *callipers* – compasses
[3] *sinuations* – waves
[4] *pivoted* – turned
[5] *teal . . . mallard* – types of duck
[6] *inviolate* – unharmed
[7] *fuselage* – body of the plane
[8] *fidelity* – loyalty, faithfulness

In the Gentle Afternoon
Royston Ellis *Dominica*

Such commerce
for a small village without a representative
on Central Government, without a village council,
without a working public toilet, with two
5 stand pipes, three rum shops and a cricket pitch;
such business
as citizens sit on benches and discuss
the latest test scores, last night's trouble
at the dance, Sunday's chance in the rounders match
10 the price of cod fish, the problems of cross week;
such activity
late in the afternoon on Friday as mother
rushes over to seize her child; boys plot;
a girl shouts her directions, a jeep coughs
15 to a standstill by the shop, and erupts an eager crowd;
such peace
in the gentle afternoon, as the sun begins to die
and everybody drifts away to attend their affairs
all part of the village family, all private people
20 with each a share of secrets, known by all.

The Sailor Sings Back to the Casuarinas
(from *The Schooner Flight*)
Derek Walcott *St Lucia*

You see them on the low hills of Barbados
bracing like windbreaks, needles for hurricanes,
trailing, like masts, the cirrus[1] of torn sails;
when I was green like them, I used to think
5 those cypresses[2], leaning against the sea,
that take the sea noise up into the branches,
are not real cypresses but casuarinas[3].
Now captain just call them Canadian cedars.
But cedars, cypresses, or casuarinas,

10 whoever called them so had a good cause,
    watching their bending bodies wail like women
    after a storm, when some schooner came home
    with news of one more sailor drowned again.
    Once the sound "cypress" used to make more sense
15 than the green "casuarinas", though, to the wind
    whatever grief bent them was all the same,
    since they were trees with nothing else in mind
    but heavenly leaping or to guard a grave;
    but we live like our names and you would have
20 to be colonial to know the difference,
    to know the pain of history words contain,
    to love those trees with an inferior love,
    and to believe: "Those casuarinas bend
    like cypresses, their hair hangs down in rain
25 like sailors' wives. They're classic trees, and we,
    if we live like the names our masters please,
    by careful mimicry⁴ might become men."

¹ *cirrus* – kind of cloud
² *cypresses* – trees like tall cones
³ *casuarinas* – trees with tiny leaves or branches that look like horses' tails
⁴ *mimicry* – aping, copying

Allegre
Derek Walcott *St Lucia*

Some mornings are as full of elation¹
As these pigeons crossing the hill slopes,
Silver as they veer in sunlight and white
On the warm blue shadows of the range.
5 And the sunward sides of the shacks
Gilded,² as though this was Italy.

The bird's claws fasten round the lignum-vitae,
The roots of delight growing downward,
As the singer in his prime.

10 And the slopes of the forest this sunrise
Are thick with blue haze, as the colour
Of the woodsmoke from the first workman's fire.
A morning for wild bees and briersmoke,
For hands cupped to boys' mouths, the holloa
15 Of their cries in the cup of the valley.
The stream keeps its edges, wind-honed,
As the intellect is clear in affections,
Calm, with the rivulet's diligence.

Men are sawing with the wind on those ridges,
20 Trees arching, campeche³, gommiers, canoe-wood³,
The sawn trunks trundled down hillsides
To crash to the edge of the sea.
No temples, yet the fruits of intelligence,
No roots, yet the flowers of identity,
25 No cities, but white seas in sunlight,
Laughter and doves, like young Italy.

Yet to find the true self is still arduous,⁴
And for us, especially, the elation can be useless and empty
As this pale, blue ewer of the sky,
30 Loveliest in drought.

¹ *elation* – joy, gladness
² *gilded* – covered in gold
³ *campeche, gommiers, cane-wood* – trunks of trees
⁴ *arduous* – hard, difficult

Discussion and Activities

Rampanalgas p147

1 'squid' (l 3) are like octopuses. Why, do you imagine, do the palm trees seem like hefted (lifted) squid to the 'I' in the poem? Where is he/she? Who is said to 'print near this beach hut the one word/Home.' (l 9)? How do you know when the beach hut was built?

2 What do you suppose was 'the heart's first effort' (l 11)? Why do you think it was described that way? How do you think the 'I' was affected when he/she saw it 'rusting shut' (l 11)? What thoughts do you imagine in the 'I's mind when he/she says 'and turn from the glass' (l 12)?

3 Do you see any symbolism in lines 13-14? How do 'trees' (l 13) and 'falls back' (l 14) fit the thoughts about 'Rust' (l 1), 'one more look' (l 2), 'years later' (l 10), and so on?

Dry Season Nights p147

1 This poem seems to have been written by a visitor to Trinidad at Carnival time. Why do you think the 'I' was 'Pink by sunset' (l 17)? What do you imagine the 'afterglow' (l 18) to be? Why do you suppose an 'insect coil' (l 20) was lit?

2 What had happened when the speaker in the poem was approached by jab-jabs in the carnival? What was 'regretted' (l 12) about the incident? Why do you think the speaker says 'whose worst weapon is a hug' (l 14)?

3 Why do you suppose that when the speaker wakes 'at one or two' (l 1) certain things make him/her 'remember/other friendships gone like water from a saucer' (l 7-8)? What does he/she see and hear then?

4 The speaker tells of what he/she 'regretted' (l 12). Would you say there is more than regret expressed in the poem? What suggests that?

At Home the Green Remains p148

1 In temperate countries leaves of trees turn yellow, red, gold and similar colours in autumn. Where is the 'I' speaking from? Which

limbs are seen as 'black limbs' (l 3)? Can you imagine why?

2   New England is in north-eastern United States. Why do you suppose the 'I' goes from England to New England? What is said about the trees in autumn? What to the 'I' appears as 'ruined temples' (l 8)?

3   'At home the green remains'. Which green? How do 'palm' (l 9) and 'poinsettias' (l 12) tell the reader where 'I's home is? What is said to 'tack', But late, the yearly notice' (ll 13-14)? What meaning do you give to the phrase, 'the yearly notice'? Why do you suppose the 'I' said 'splendid' (l 12)? Is there any other evidence in lines 9-14 about how the 'I' feels about home?

Welsh Landscape p149

1   'You cannot live in the present' (l 11). What do you take that to mean? How is it connected with 'spilled blood' (l 2), 'style' (l 9), and 'sped arrows' (l 10)? Would you agree that lines 22-23 contain what the whole poem is about? Say why or why not.

2   What imagery, if any, comes to your mind with a) 'the wild sky' (l 3)'; b) 'thick ambush of shadows' (l 18); c) 'wind-bitten towers and castles' (l 24); d) 'mouldering quarries and mines' (l 26)?

3   Impotent (l 27) means powerless. Why do you suppose the speaker in the poem speaks of 'an impotent people' (l 27)? Impotent in what way? How would you interpret the last line of the poem?

4   What tone or mood do you hear in the voice of the speaker in the poem? Try to say why you hear it.

Islands p150

1   What islands are these? What do those who hate the islands see? What do those with delight in their eyes see?

2   Put into your own words the comment or observation made in lines 20-23; also the meaning of lines 46-55. What reasons does the poet give for saying what he does in lines 46-55?

3   What meaning do you see in the imagery of lines 28-32?

4   What would you say is the tone or mood of this poem or the attitude of the poet? Why do you say so?

There is a Mystic Splendour p151

1   The 'Brethren of the Coast' (l 10) were pirates and buccaneers of the 17th century, and 'privateers' (l 9) were ships' captains looking to

plunder the wealth of the Caribbean. Can you explain why their activities were connected to a) 'ancient vessels' (l 4); b) 'martial shouting' (l 6); c) 'cannons thundered' (l 7); d) 'black battle haze' (l 7); e) 'buried treasure chests' (l 16); f) 'Morgan's gold' (l 16)?

2   'Walking this shore' (l 2). When? What is heard? Do the palm trees 'murmur' (l 15). What do they do? To say that trees 'murmur' is a metaphor that has been overused. Are there others?

3   Why do you suppose the speaker in the poem feels 'a mystic splendour' (l 1) – an enrichment of his spirit? What kind of feeling do you hear in the tone of voice of the speaker? Do you think it is there because he thinks that is how he is supposed to feel, that is, 'poetic'? Or because he genuinely feels something when he is in that place? Explain why you hold your point of view.

Leaving Home p152

1   These lines come from the booklength poem *Another Life* from which the lines called *In My Fourteenth Year* (p117) were also taken. The 'Morne' (l 2) is a hill in Castries, St. Lucia. Seawell (l 46) was the name of the airport in Barbados. Where was the 'I' when he 'watched the island narrowing' (l 33)? Which island? Why was he there? When? Who were 'the three faces I had most dearly loved that year' (l 29)? What does 'Jamaica just up the road, man' (l 31) tell you? Why do you think a young man of nineteen left St Lucia to go to Jamaica?

2   What is suggested about St Lucia's history in lines 13-14? Teal and mallard are birds of the north. What is meant in line 16? What is being said there about the island? How would you interpret 'There was no history. No memory' (l 19) when you put it with line 14? What is mourned in line 20?

3   In lines 33-42 the 'I' describes being on the plane. What imagery enters your mind as you read them? Are any of the metaphors ones you met before in any poem you have read?

4   This poet's works are enjoyed because from his powerful imagination he produces fresh, rich, memorable metaphors. Some people nowadays think such use of metaphors is a fault, either because they do not have strong imaginations or because they think metaphors are too 'poetic'. Yet ordinary people use many metaphors in everyday life. Which camp would you be inclined to join, and why?

In the Gentle Afternoon p154

1 The speaker says 'commerce' (l 1), 'business' (l 6), 'activity' (l 11).
   What is he/she observing going on in the small village? What are
   you made to imagine with a) 'standpipes' (l 5); b) 'rum shops' (l 5);
   c) 'cricket pitch' (l 5); d) 'on benches and discuss' (l 7); e) 'late in
   the afternoon on Friday' (l 12); f) 'a jeep coughs to a standstill'
   (ll 14-15); g) 'erupts an eager crowd' (l 15)? What topics of
   conversation fill the villagers' lives?

2 When the speaker says 'peace' (l 16), What is he/she thinking of?
   What kind of picture or image comes to you with a) 'the sun begins
   to die' (l 17); b) 'drifts away' (l 18)? Does the phrase 'in the gentle
   afternoon' (l 17) suggest any particular kind of feeling to you? If so,
   what kind?

3 The villagers are described as 'all part of the village family' (l 19).
   How does the last line of the poem make that real? What attitude to
   village life is being communicated by the poem?

The Sailor Sings Back to the Casuarinas p154

1 What do you think 'when I was green' (l 4) means? Does the person
   have the same opinions now as when he was green? What is it the
   'I' 'used to think' (l 4) of casuarinas, which are like trees called
   cypresses in northern countries?

2 Why do you suppose he had the word 'real' (l 7) in mind? If
   something is not real, it is false. So in what way in the 'I's mind
   were the casuarinas false? What, then, for him when he was green,
   was genuine or real? Where did something have to belong to be
   genuine, in his 'green' mind? What did he think of its quality if it
   belonged to a place like Barbados?

3 Which lines or phrases reveal to you that now that he is no longer
   'green' the 'I' sees casuarinas, cypresses, and Canadian cedars as all
   the same? What does he associate their 'bending bodies' (l 11) with?

4 'to love those trees with an inferior love' (l 52). Which trees? Does
   that lead you to think that when Shabine went to school in St Lucia
   in the 1930s and 1940s he was made to think that certain things
   had an inferior value? Which things? Trees? Anything else? With
   your knowledge of West Indian history, why do you suppose that
   happened? Even now some West Indians speak of spring and
   autumn as if they are better seasons than ours. What do you

imagine as 'the pain of history words contain' (l 21)?

5   The speaker quotes words from someone else in lines 23-27. Why
    do you suppose he quotes something about 'our masters' (l 26) and
    'mimicry' (l 27) (blind copying, imitation?)

Allegre p155

1   In old Italian paintings the colour of gold was used a lot. Why do
    you think the shacks are said to be 'Gilded as though this was Italy'
    (l 6)? What are 'these pigeons' (l 2) doing? Sometimes when 'a
    singer in his prime' (l 9) is seen, the veins in the neck stand out like
    cords. Can you think why the singing bird (ll 7-9) reminds the
    speaker of that? What comes from the 'workman's fire' (l 21)?

2   Why, do you imagine, is 'the intellect' (l 17) – the mind – compared
    to 'The stream' (l 16)? Why do you think the words 'clear' (l 17) and
    'diligence' (l 18) are used? Whose mind might be the one 'honed'
    (l 16) – sharp, 'clear' and diligent that morning?

3   Which place do you suppose is said to have 'No cities, but white
    seas in sunlight' (l 25)? Ancient Greece, a civilisation that had great
    importance in history, had many beautiful temples. How would you
    interpret 'No temples, but the fruits of intelligence' (l 23)? Using
    your knowledge of Caribbean history, what would you say accounts
    for its having 'No roots, but the flowers of identity' (l 24)?

4   'to find the true self' (l 27). What do you suppose is meant by 'the
    true self' when you think of 'the flowers of identity'? Why does the
    speaker say finding it is 'arduous' – very difficult – although there
    are 'flowers of identity'? What have the 'flowers' to become?

5   The speaker began with 'Some mornings are full of elation' (l 1) a
    feeling of joy and gladness – and the poem is called *Allegre* (a
    cheerful time), but then says 'for us, especially, the elation can be
    useless and empty'. How do you see the regret there related to
    finding 'the true self'? Could the speaker be talking about himself
    and finding his own true self, his own identity, his own way of
    producing 'the fruits of intelligence'? Could the 'us' (l 28) be 'me'?

6   Identify why there is irony in having a blue sky, which suggests
    comfort and enjoyment, at the time of 'drought' (l 30). What is the
    discouragment being expressed in 'Loveliest in drought'? Poets
    sometimes have periods of drought. Again, could the elation be
    'useless and empty' because the poet is struggling with something?
    What became lovely in his drought?

The Woman Speaks to the Man who has Employed Her Son
Lorna Goodison   *Jamaica*

Her son was first made known to her
as a sense of unease, a need to cry
for little reasons and a metallic tide
rising in her mouth each morning.
5   Such signs made her know
that she was not alone in her body.
She carried him full term
tight up under her heart.

She carried him like the poor
10   carry hope, hope you get a break
or a visa, hope one child go through
and remember you. He had no father.
The man she made him with had more
like him, he was fair-minded
15   he treated all his children
with equal absolute indifference.

She raised him twice, once as mother
then as father, set no ceiling
on what he could be: doctor
20   earth healer, pilot take wings.
But now he tells her he is working
for you, that you value him so much
you give him one whole submachine gun
for him alone.

25   He says you are like a father to him
she is wondering what kind of father
would give a son hot and exploding
death when he asks him for bread.

She went downtown and bought three
30   and one third yards of black cloth

And a deep crowned and veiled hat
for the day he draw his bloody salary.

she has no power over you and this
at the level of earth, what she has
35 are prayers and a mother's tears
and at knee city she uses them.

she says psalms for him
she reads psalms for you
she weeps for his soul
40 her eyewater covers you.

She is throwing a partner[1]
with Judas Iscariot's mother
the thief on the left-hand side
of the cross, his mother

45 is the banker, her draw though
is first and last for she still
throwing two hands as mother and father
she is prepared, she is done. Absalom.

[1] *a partner* – Called a sou-sou in some islands. A group of persons subscribe a certain amount weekly or monthly to a fund. Each week or month one person draws the sum.

No Man's Land
Gloria Escoffery *Jamaica*

The body of a fourteen year old caught playing politics
Makes a hummock[1] on the ground beside his ratchet knife
Which drew blood but cannot bleed for him.
The muzzle of a sawn-off shotgun masks the eye of one
5 Who, being a man (?), thinks himself a great gun.
The gully scrub[2] cannot hide him forever;
Silenced, he drops the gun and becomes a dead man.

Now the killer's 'baby mother' is caught by the press photographer;
For the morning paper and forever she throws up her arms
10 In the traditional gesture of prayer.
Wai oh! Aie! Eheu! mourns the camera shot matron
Whose stringy son, like a sucked mango seed,
Lies there no more use to anyone;
Soon to be inseparable from the rest of the levelled ground.
15 Why this pieta³ needs to be enacted in our land
No one can explain:
It clearly belongs within the pieties of a museum frame.
Is there no way but through this scene?

¹ *hummock* – mound, lump
² *scrub* – bushes
³ *pieta* – picture or sculpture of the Virgin Mary holding the dead body of Christ

Theophilus Jones Walks Naked Down King Street
Heather Royes   *Jamaica*

On Monday, October 18th,
Theophilus Jones took off
his asphalt-black, rag-tag pants
and walked naked down King Street.
5 It was a holiday –
and only a few people saw
his triumphant march,
his muscular, bearded-brown body,
his genitals flapping in front.
10 Theophilus Jones had wanted
to do this for a long time.

At Tower and King, three carwash boys
shouting "Madman!", followed him to Harbour Street,
but seeing his indifference, turned
15 and dribbled back up the road.
Down on the Ferry Pier, a handful of people

waiting for the boat, stared out to sea
but did not see
Theophilus enter the water.

20 He walked out as far as possible,
then began to swim, strongly and calmly,
into the middle of the harbour.
Eventually, way out in the deep,
he stopped,

25 floated for a while, enjoying the sun,
watched a plane take off from the green-rimmed palisades,
and then, letting himself go,
allowed the water
to swallow him up.

30 Theophilus Jones went down
slowly,
slowly his bent legs, slowly
his arms above his head,
slowly his locksed[1] hair,

35 slowly.
Until nothing could be seen of him.
Some orange peel, an old tin-can
and a sea-saturated[2] cigarette box
floated over his demise,[3]

40 while nearby,
a kingfisher – scavenging for sprats
on a low current – veered down
and landed,
in a spray of sunlit water.

[1] *locksed* – braided or plaited and matted
[2] *saturated* – soaked
[3] *demise* – death

5 Ways to Kill a Man
Edwin Brock   *England*

There are many cumbersome ways to kill a man
you can make him carry a plank of wood
to the top of a hill and nail him to it. To do this
properly you require a crowd of people
5 wearing sandals, a cock that crows, a cloak
to dissect, a sponge, some vinegar and one
man to hammer the nails home.

Or you can take a length of steel,
shaped and chased in a traditional way,
10 and attempt to pierce the metal cage he wears.
But for this you need white horses,
English trees, men with bows and arrows,
at least two flags, a prince and a
castle to hold your banquet in.

15 Dispensing with[1] nobility, you may, if the wind
allows, blow gas at him. But then you need
a mile of mud sliced through with ditches,
not to mention black boots, bomb craters,
more mud, a plague of rats, a dozen songs
20 and some round hats made of steel.

In an age of aeroplanes, you may fly
miles above your victim and dispose of him by
pressing one small switch. All you then
require is an ocean to separate you, two
25 systems of government, a nation's scientists,
several factories, a psychopath[2] and
land that no one needs for several years.

These are, as I began, cumbersome ways
to kill a man. Simpler, direct, and much more neat
30 is to see that he is living somewhere in the middle
of the twentieth century, and leave him there.

[1] *dispensing with* – putting aside, omitting, not considering
[2] *psychopath* – a violent, mentally ill person who kills for pleasure

No Cowries

Christine Craig *Jamaica*

No cowries[1]
no pretty bangles
any more.

The cripple in the plaza
5 looking for Garvey
gave up long ago on smiles,
hunts in abuse.

Our eyes have grown
as empty as our bellies,
10 sulky in our bankrupt[2]
anger we trade in hate.

It must count that
a brother has made
a booth, knitted colour
15 on a moving street.

It must matter
that another weaves
parlour chairs by
busy afro lights.

20 To win our own smiles
to gain our own nods
still so much begging
time left, friend?

[1] *cowries* – shells, commonly worn as decoration
[2] *bankrupt* – unproductive

Colonial Girls' School
Olive Senior   *Jamaica*

Borrowed images
willed[1] our skins pale
muffled our laughter
lowered our voices
5 let out our hems
dekinked our hair
denied our sex in gym tunics and bloomers
harnessed our voices to madrigals[2]
and genteel airs
10 yoked our minds to declensions in Latin
and the language of Shakespeare

Told us nothing about ourselves
There was nothing about us at all

How those pale northern eyes and
15 aristocratic whispers once erased us
How our loudness, our laughter
debased us

There was nothing left of ourselves
Nothing about us at all

20 Studying *History Ancient and Modern*
Kings and Queens of England
Steppes of Russia
Wheatfields of Canada

There was nothing of our landscape there
25 Nothing about us at all

Marcus Garvey turned twice in his grave.
Thirty-eight[3] was a beacon. A flame.
They were talking of desegregation[4]
in Little Rock, Arkansas. Lumumba
30 and the Congo. To us: mumbo-jumbo.

We had read Vachel Lindsay's[5]
vision of the jungle

Feeling nothing about ourselves
There was nothing about us at all

35 Months, years, a childhood memorising
Latin declensions
(For our language
'bad talking' –
detentions)

40 Finding nothing about us there
Nothing about us at all

So, friend of my childhood years
One day we'll talk about
How the mirror broke
45 Who kissed us awake
Who let Anansi from his bag

For isn't it strange how
northern eyes
in the brighter world before us now

50 Pale?

[1] *willed* – wished
[2] *madrigals* – English songs
[3] *'Thirty-eight'* – 1938
[4] *desegregation* – stopping separation of people by race
[5] *Vachel Lindsay* – American poet who wrote the poem *The Congo*

Ocho Rios
Lorna Goodison   *Jamaica*

A conquistador[1] hit by the muse[2] who gives names
tongue-tied eight rivers together.
The British, recognising that the Spaniards

had the all-time hit "Arawak Genocide",
5   let that name be. But wrought[3] some name-calling
of their own.

"so how black, black man like you and me
name Goodison and Montgomery?"

In Ocho Rios market I ask the cookshop lady

10   "how much for the curry goat?"
"Three dolla"
"Fi wan curry goat?"
"A four dolla fi tourist sista".

I beat her down to a dollar fifty.
15   she says I am clearly roots.[4]
I tell her the curry goat irie.[5]

It's true. Its taste strokes my senses gone wild from smells
astringent[6] vegetables and heaps of earth wrapped yams.
The crotchety old maid selling lace and the one from St Mary,
20   Face oiled with Necromancy[7], selling asophetida and mustard yellow
sulphur and Kananga Water and frankincense and myrrh.

The sign in the square says "Tourism, not socialism"
and though I eat this curry sitting on a feed bag from Florida

This market belies[8] your investments Isabella[9]
25   And you Combulous, whose aims conjuncted with Venn and
       Penables,[10]
which Colonizer[11] is winning in Ocho Rios?

[1]   *conquistador* – Spanish conqueror
[2]   *muse* – goddess
[3]   *wrought* – did
[4]   *roots* – of the people of the place
[5]   *irie* – is of the best
[6]   *astringent* – sharp
[7]   *Necromancy* – talking with the spirit of the dead
[8]   *beliefs* – negates, discredits
[9]   *Isabella* – queen of Spain who sent Columbus
[10]   *Venn and Penables* – humorous alteration of Penn and Venables, Englishmen
     who captured Jamaica from the Spanish
[11]   *Colonizer* – one who takes over a country for his own profit

Limbo Dancer at Immigration
John Agard   *Guyana*

It was always the same
at every border/at every frontier/
at every port/at every airport/
of every metropolis

5 The same hassle[1]
from authorities

the same battle
with bureaucrats[2]

a bunch of official cats
10 ready to scratch
looking limbo dancer up & down
scrutinising passport with a frown

COUNTRY OF ORIGIN: SLAVESHIP

Never heard of that one
15 the authorities sniggered

Suppose you got here on a banana boat
the authorities sniggered

More like a spaceship
the authorities sniggered

20 Slaveship/spaceship/Pan Am/British Airways/Air France
It's all the same
smiled limbo dancer

Now don't give us any of your lip
the authorities sniggered

25 ANY IDENTIFYING MARKS?

And when limbo dancer showed them sparks
of vision in eyes that held rivers
it meant nothing to them

And when limbo dancer held up hands
30   that told a tale of nails
it meant nothing to them

And when limbo dancer offered a neck
that bore the brunt of countless lynchings
it meant nothing to them
35   And when limbo dancer revealed ankles
bruised with the memory of chains
it meant nothing to them

So limbo dancer bent over backwards
& danced
40   & danced
& danced

until from every limb
flowed a trail of red

& what the authorities thought
45   was a trail of blood

was only spilt duty-free wine

so limbo dancer smiled
saying I have nothing to declare

& to the sound of drums disappeared

¹ *bureaucrats* – government officials
² *lynchings* – unlawful hangings

The Hand That Signed the Paper
Dylan Thomas   *Wales*

The hand that signed the paper felled[1] a city;
Five sovereign[2] fingers taxed the breath,
Doubled the globe of dead and halved a country;
These five kings did a king to death.

5   The mighty hand leads to a sloping shoulder,
The finger joints are cramped with chalk;
A goose's quill[3] has put an end to murder
That put an end to talk.

The hand that signed the treaty bred a fever,
10 And famine grew, and locusts came;
Great is the hand that holds dominion over
Man by a scribbled name.

The five kings count the dead but do not soften
The crusted wound nor stroke the brow;
15 A hand rules pity as a hand rules heaven;
Hands have no tears to flow.

[1] *felled* defeated, destroyed, ruined
[2] *sovereign* – ruling as a king
[3] *quill* – end of feather used as a pen

Embassy
W.H. Auden   *England*

As evening fell the day's oppression[1] lifted;
Far peaks came into focus; it had rained:
Across wide lawns and cultured flowers drifted
The conversation of the highly trained.

5   Two gardeners watched them pass and priced their shoes;
A chauffeur waited, reading in the drive,
For them to finish their exchange of views;
It seemed a picture of the private life.

Far off, no matter what good they intended,
10   The armies waited for a verbal error
With all the instruments for causing pain:

And on the issue of their charm depended
A land laid waste, with all its young men slain,
Its women weeping, and its towns in terror.

¹ *oppression* – dark weather

Skeete's Bay, Barbados.
Robert Lee   *St Lucia*

One always missed the turning, but found, in time
The broken sign that pointed crookedly, loathe¹ to
Allow another stranger here. Perhaps this Tom
Or Dick has plans for progress that will tow
5   The boats away and make them 'quaint'; that will tame
This wild coast with pale rheumatics who tee

Off² where sea-egg shells and fishermen
Now lie with unconcern. Naked children
And their sticks flush crabs from out their holes
10   And a bare legged girl, dress in wet folds
Wades slow towards a waning sun.

And the sea tossed angrily
For it knew that freedom here was short.
It remembered other coasts
15   Made mod by small-eyed men in big cars.
And, as before, it knew she'd vanish
The bare legged girl; the children and their crabs
Would leave; a better world would banish
Them to imitation coconut trays.
20   But those small eyes reflecting dollar signs
Have not yet found the crooked finger to this peace;
And down the beach the women bathe their sons

Who'll never talk, like Pap, of fishing seasons past.
Only memory will turn down this way
5 When some old man somewhere recalls his day
On this beach where sea-egg shells once lay.

Lessons
Kingsley Amis   *England*

How long, when hand of master is withdrawn,
Will hand of pupil move as is it stayed?
The books once closed, the classroom blind run down,
Who thinks of lessons now there is no need?

5 Docility¹, of feature or of mind,
Is glad to wither when the tongue is free;
Even if one phrase, one shared thought, remained,
Ten more will come and go by half past four.

Therefore let all who teach discard² this pride,
10 That anything is learnt except to please;
When fingers touch, or how love's names are said,
Like any lessons, change with time and place;
So here and now, with individual care,
This one sole way hand may be laid on hand,
15 Voice only with one voice may learn to cry,
And thus tongue lie with tongue, thus mind with
   mind.

But out of school, all ways the hand will move,
Forget the private hour, and touch the world;
The voice will bawl, slur the accent of love,
20 The tongue slop sweets, the mind lounge home
   expelled.

¹ *docility* – meekness
² *discard* – throw away

Formal Application

"The poets apparently want to rejoin the human race." TIME

Donald W. Baker   *USA*

I shall begin by learning to throw
the knife, first at trees, until it sticks
in the trunk and quivers every time;

next from a chair, using only wrist
5 and fingers, at a thing on the ground,
a fresh ant hill or a fallen leaf;

then at a moving object, perhaps
a pieplate swinging on twine, until
I pot it at least twice in three tries.

10 Meanwhile, I shall be teaching the birds
that the skinny fellow in sneakers
is a source of suet and bread crumbs,
first putting them on a shingle nailed
to a pine tree, next scattering them
15 on the needles, closer and closer

to my seat, until the proper bird,
a towhee, I think, in black and rust
and gray, takes tossed crumbs six feet away.

Finally, I shall coordinate[2]
20 conditioned reflex[3] and functional
form and qualify as Modern Man.

You see the splash of blood and feathers
and the blade pinning it to the tree?
It's called an "Audubon Crucifix."

25 The phrase has pleasing (even pious)
connotations, like "Arbeit Macht Frei",[4]
"Molotov Cocktail",[5] and *Enola Gay*.[6]

A White Man Considers the Situation

Ian McDonald   *Trinidad and Tobago*

Perhaps it is time to retreat from these well-loved shores.
The swell heaves on the beach, angry clouds pile:
The surf is ominous,[1] storms are coming.
I see I am a tourist in my own land:
5 My brutal tenancy is over, they all say,
The centuries have faded like a dream . . .

Every day it is harder for the timid to make plans,
People do not say good morning with the former politeness
The pavements feel safe only when old men pass.
10 The grip of power slides away, slides.
Something is missing in days still filled with pleasure;
There is emptiness, dreaming in the air.
Where ruling ends, the ruler cannot stay:
A diminished[2] mastery is the keenest woe.

15 The best measure is the use of time,
My father's father planted once
A green tree in this quiet garden
It was to yield ancestral[3] wood
To grace my grandson's christening chair.
20 The best measure is the use of time.

I decorate now my dark-skinned love
With hibiscus for her shining hair
The petals fade, the sun burns out
Red hibiscus in her shining hair.

25 I lie sleepless in the embroidered sheets,
A sprig of khus-khus scents the room.
The night is dark with cloud, and lonely.
The black sentries are whispering restless.
My father heard a hurricane of nightingales
30 Once upon a time, once upon a time.
Now the owl hoots, signalling danger coming
The moon is half alight, throwing coldness.

There is no way back, no forward way:
My heart grows clenched with inner grief.
35 Almost certainly I will have to go from here.
The laagers⁴ of the world build higher, black and white.
And no one is to blame except my brother, me.
No one is to blame except my brother.

¹ *ominous* – like a bad omen of origin
² *diminished* – lessened
³ *ancestral* – passed down generations of the same family
⁴ *laagers* – fenced camps defended against others

The Islander

Clovis Scott   *Bermuda*

Cooped up in his walled-in cottage, he circles
The route from his school, hotel or job to his home,
In a routine which has few variations.

Born in a ward shut off for his skin,
5 Reared in a school vested in his caste,¹
And taking his pay from forty thieves,

He climbs the hill to his house in very slow steps,
His eyes fixed downwards like a nail to the wall,
His feet trained from birth to crawl on the ground;

10 Wed to the first girl that he kisses at home,
Who is marked out for him in their separate compound,
Forbidden to ask himself what he is and will be

Aside from the pay of his work and his nature,
Held by the pace of his friends everywhere,
15 The chains of history drag his feet in all things;

All of his customs gauged to the foreign tourists,
Every luxury that he owns is bought by permission:
The greenest of islands is the tightest of cages.

¹ *caste* – rigid social class

Girl Reporter
Philip Hobsbaum   *England*

Fact is her fiction. Sitting in a bar
Raincoat still on, crossed nylon legs revealing
Less than we think, a male in tow and smiling
Her narrowed eyes flick past to register
5 Whether I am a story¹ in the offing.²

Life is material for her creation.
The doll by the up-turned scooter – that is real,
Its head, see, stains the kerb. She runs to call
The news desk first, then after the police-station,
10 Already mapping the story of the trial.

Errors of fact are part of her prose style.
With every slashing cross-head³ some truth dies.
In love? She knows. You hate her? She knows.
    You'll
Cure cancer? Reach the moon? Her face may smile –
15 You're placed by those all-knowing know-all eyes.
We're butterflies pinned down by this young lady,
Facts of our lives are melted down for cliche.⁴
Even as I write her gaze observes my tremor –
Her lethal⁵ pencil always at the ready.

¹ *story* – news item
² *in the offing* – likely to happen soon
³ *cross-head* – a paragraph heading
⁴ *cliche* – stale, overused phrase or idea
⁵ *lethal* – deadly, fatal

Discussion and Activities

The Woman Speaks To The Man Who Has Employed Her Son p162

1 How did the woman first know she was pregnant? What do you take 'he had no father' (l 22) to mean? What do lines 15-18 tell about what the mother had to do? Why did she have to carry her son 'like the poor carry hope' (ll 9-10)? Why is a 'visa' (l 11) said to be one of the hopes of the poor? How do you interpret 'set no ceiling on what he could be' (ll 18-19)? What system used by poor people to save money did the mother join?

2 But now he tells her he is working for you' (ll 21-22). Doing what? What do you suppose was the business of his employer? What do you assume would be the son's 'bloody salary' (l 32)?

3 The mother had 'set no ceiling . . . doctor . . . pilot . . .' (ll 18-20). What do you imagine her state of mind to be now? How does she prepare herself for what is to happen to her son? How do you interpret 'at knee city' (l 36)? Why is she 'throwing a partner' (l 41)? Christians would know the story of Judas Iscariot who betrayed Christ. Can you suggest why the person running the 'partner' as 'the banker' (l 45) is referred to as 'Judas Iscariot's mother'?

4 Which of these would you say the words 'she is prepared, she is done' (l 48) contain? – a) satisfaction; b) indifference; c) hopelessness; d) anger. Do you think the mother represents others or is she a special case? If she represents others, who are they? What do you think was the intention of the poet in making this poem? Why? How does it make you feel? What cry is it making? Does *5 Ways to Kill a Man* (p166) share anything with this poem?

No Man's Land p163

1 In Jamaica at one time political rivalry caused violence between gangs. A hummock is a piece of rising ground. Why does the boy's body make 'a hummock on the ground' (l 2)? Why do you think it is said the 14-year-old was caught 'playing politics' (l 1)? Who do you suppose is 'the killer's 'baby mother'' (l 8)? How is she 'caught by a press photographer' (l 8)? What meaning do you give to 'camera shot' (l 11)? Whose arms were thrown up in 'the traditional gesture of prayer' (l 10)?

2 How would you interpret line 14? What is on the ratchet knife? Why is it said it 'cannot bleed for him' (l 3)? Who was 'silenced and becomes a dead man' (l 7)? Why is it said 'the gully scrub cannot hide him forever' (l 6)? Why do you suppose a question mark in brackets is put after 'man' in line 5?

3 A pieta is a picture or sculpture of the Virgin Mary holding the dead body of Christ on her lap or in her arms. What 'pieta' is meant in line 15? Why do you think the speaker says 'No one can explain' (l 16)? In a museum pictures and things of the past are kept. Why do you suppose the speaker says line 17? How would you interpret 'Is there no way but through this scene?' (l 18)?

4 Which of these tones of voice comes through to you from the poem? Say how; a) sarcasm; b) annoyance; c) sorrow; d) playfulness.

Theophilus Jones Walks Naked Down King Street p164

1 How soon do you realise Theophilus is a vagrant? Did anyone take any notice of him? Why, do you imagine, he entered the water and 'allowed the water to swallow him up' (ll 28-29)? Do you think he did not know what he was doing? Why then had he 'wanted to do this for a long time' (l 11)? Walking naked was an act of defiance and disrespect. What do you suppose he was defiant about?

2 Did anyone care about his defiance? His walk is called a 'triumphant march' (l 7). Did Theophilus score a victory of any kind? While he was giving up his life, how was life going on as usual around him?

3 How are his walk and his slow death described in lines 30-36 like a ritual sacrifice? What contrasts are used to make the sacrifice stand out clearly? What contrasting associations are aroused by 'orange peel', 'an old tin-can', 'cigarette box' and 'scavenging' (ll 37-41)? Are those images used to make you laugh or to suggest the status and treatment of people like Theophilus?

4 Is he bring regarded as a fool and a nuisance, or as a victim of the people amongst whom he was living? Is his death meant to represent an event of tragic irony or just an act of madness? What is the feeling the poet wants to arouse about people like Theophilus? Is the poem full of sentimentality (excessive feeling about something that does not merit it), and did the poet write it like that because that is how one is supposed to feel about such people? Or is the feeling quite genuine?

1 Which killing that Christians know of is associated with 'a cock that crows' (l 5), 'a sponge, some vinegar' (l 6), and 'one man to hammer the nails home' (l 7)? In which time of history did that killing take place? Were other men also killed like that at the time?

2 During which time did men wear what is described in the poem as 'a metal cage' (l 10)? Have you ever seen films or pictures of those times? What do you think is called 'a length of steel' (l 8)? Who might have ridden 'white horses' (l 11)? Which men used 'bows and arrows' (l 12) then with the men on the horses? For what purpose? What is the method for killing a man then that the poem refers to?

3 In what was called the Great War (1914-1918) poison gas was used for the first time to kill soldiers in the trenches of the battlefields. What do you think 'mud' (l 17), 'ditches' (l 17), and 'rats' (l 19) had to do with that war? Who do you imagine wore 'black boots' (l 18)? Who do you suppose wore 'round hats made of steel' (l 20)? Why? Which way of killing men came into use then?

4 What would you say is meant by 'dispose of him' (l 22)? Who is called 'your victim' (l 22)? What do you think aeroplanes had to do with victims? How were victims disposed of by 'pressing one small switch' (l 23)? Two atomic bombs destroyed two cities in Japan in 1945 and left poisonous radiation for many years. Why do you think the speaker says 'land that no one needs for several years' (l 27)? Who do you suppose the speaker refers to as a 'psychopath' (l 26)? Is it one particular person or anyone who does certain things? Which things does the speaker have in mind? What is he or she then saying about people who declare war on others? Why are 'scientists' (l 25) and 'factories' (l 26) involved? Which way of killing is dealt with then in lines 21-27?

5 How does the speaker say that just living in today's world is more of a death-threat than anything he/she mentioned before? Why do you suppose he/she thinks that? Does any idea here remind you of the poem *The Woman Speaks To The Man Who Has Employed Her Son* (p162)? What do you think the speaker in this poems means by saying 'it is simpler, direct and much more neat' (l 29)? What is his/her tone of voice in saying those things? Does the tone of voice change in lines 28-31, or not? What strong attitude to what is happening in the world comes out of the poem? How similar or different it is to the attitude in *Christ Climbed Down* (p134)?

No Cowries p167

1 Cowries are shells which were worn by African women as ornaments, and sometimes used as money. Why do you suppose the speaker speaks of 'No cowries' (l 1) as a Jamaican woman?

2 Marcus Garvey (l 5) was a Jamaican whose name was known in the 1930s and 1940s all over the world as a leader who wanted to get all people of African descent in the Caribbean and North America back to Africa. What reason or reasons could the cripple in the plaza have had for 'looking for Garvey' (l 5)? Is the name Garvey used to mean a living person, or as a symbol for the cripple's thoughts? Why do you suppose he 'gave up long ago' (l 6)? Gave up what? How do you interpret 'hunts in abuse' (l 7)?

3 'We trade in hate' (l 11). Who do you think does that in the poem? What reason is given for it? Who is meant by 'a brother' (l 13)? What do you think he 'made a booth' (ll 13-14) to do? What has 'another' (l 17) done?

4 What meaning do you give to lines 20-21? Why do you think the speaker in the poem says 'It must matter' (l 16)? Why the question: 'so much begging time left, friend?' (ll 22-24)? What would you say is the attitude of the speaker to eyes that 'have grown as empty as our bellies' (ll 8-9), to 'abuse' (l 7), to 'trade in hate' (l 11)?

Colonial Girls' School p168

1 'Colonial' refers to the time when places in the West Indies were British colonies and were controlled from Britain. Whose skins are 'our skins' (l 2)? Where were their minds 'yoked' (l 10)? What do lines 12-13 tell you about the lessons taught in class? Some English songs are 'madrigals' (l 8). Why were their voices 'harnessed' to madrigals? Whose were the 'pale northern eyes' (l 14)?

2 How do you interpret 'willed our skins pale' (l 2)? Who do you think had that wish? What do you suppose were 'Borrowed images' (l 1)? How does that fit in with lines 18-19, 24-25, 33-34? What were they instructed to do in lines 3-9 to be like the 'Borrowed images'? What was the local dialect said to be?

3 'Thirty-eight' (l 27) refers to 1938 when protests began against how local people, especially those called 'the workers', were being treated. Which persons and places connected with those protests are referred to in lines 26-30?

4 The word 'pale' is used in a literal sense in line 14, but in a metaphorical sense in line 50. What does it mean in each case? Why is it said that 'northern eyes . . . now/Pale' (ll 48-50)? Discuss why the poet used words like 'muffled', 'denied', 'harnessed', 'yoked'. Would you agree that this poem is a celebration of liberation? If so, liberation from what? What does it have in common with *A Sailor Sings Back to the Casuarinas* (p154)? Do you think it differs from that poem in its tone, feeling or attitude?

Ocho Rios p169

1 In Spanish, 'Ocho Rios' means eight rivers. Who then was 'A conquistador' (l 1)? What name-calling did he do? Genocide is the killing off of a race of people. Who committed 'Arawak Genocide' (l 4)? What different kind of name-calling did the British do with names like Goodison and Montgomery?

2 Why did the cookshop lady say the 'I' was 'clearly roots' (l 15)? Which other sellers in the market are mentioned?

3 At one time the Government in power was trying to establish socialism – a policy to have all citizens share benefits from the country's resources instead of letting a few reap great profits. Who do you think put up the sign 'Tourism, not socialism' (l 22)? Why do you suppose it is said the feed bag the 'I' was sitting on came from Florida? Why do you think Isabella, who sent Columbus on his voyages, is told 'This market belies [falsifies, contradicts, betrays] your investments' (l 24)? What were Isabella's investments? Why were they made? Who now is getting profit in the market in that place? How then does that market belie investments of colonisers?

4 Penn and Venables captured Jamaica from the Spaniards for Britain. How were the arms of Columbus 'conjuncted' (l 25) – joined – with others? How many sets of colonisers, then, are referred to in the poem? How do you interpret the irony in line 26? Is the poem about marketwomen or foreign exploiters? Support your view.

Limbo Dancer at Immigration p171

1 People in some foreign places associate black people from the Caribbean with limbo dancing, a dance ritual that spread from Trinidad throughout the Caribbean and is done to entertain tourists.

Do you think the speaker in the poem is a limbo dancer, or is the term 'limbo dancer' used to say something about certain labels and stereotypes?

2 What do you think the 'hassle from authorities' at airports and customs has to do with labels and stereotypes? Do you think it has to do with the 'race' of the speaker in the poem? Why does the speaker see them as 'scrutinizing his passport with a frown' (l 12)? Isn't that done to everybody? Is the speaker carrying a chip on his shoulder?

3 Is 'Country of Origin: Slaveship' (l 13) written anywhere, spoken, or just in the mind of the limbo dancer'? What about 'Any Identifying Marks' (l 25)? References are made to 'banana boat' (l 16) – the way emigrants used to go to Britain – to 'slaveship' (l 13), 'nails' (l 30), 'lynchings' (l 35) – the murder of black people by mobs of white Americans – and to 'chains' (l 36). Why do you suppose the 'limbo dancer' made those references? What is being referred to in lines 26-27? Why, do you think, 'it meant nothing to them' (ll 28, 31, 34 and 37) is repeated?

4 To bend over backwards is to do your very best to please someone. What could line 38 mean? How do lines 39-41 tell that the 'limbo dancer' behaved as they expected a person like him to? Why, do you imagine, did the 'dancer' think the authorities saw 'a trail of blood' (l 45)? Why did he think that would satisfy them?

5 Consider how cleverly the poet used satire and irony to make his complaint against what he saw as injustice seem a bit of amusing clowning.

The Hand That Signed the Paper p173

1 What is a 'treaty' (l 9)? Why do nations or kings usually agree to and sign treaties? In what way might a treaty be related to war? 'The five kings count the dead' (l 13). Who do you imagine as the 'five kings' (l 13)? What do they have to do with 'The hand' (l 1)? Which dead? Why did they die? What could that have to do with 'the treaty' (l 9)? Is the treaty the same as 'the paper' (l 1)? How do you interpret 'Doubled the globe of dead and halved a country' (l 3)? Why was the country 'halved'? Which 'king' do you think the five kings did 'to death' (l 4)? In what way? How is that related to *Christ Climbed Down* (p134) and in *5 Ways To Kill A Man* (p166)?

2 'A goose's quill' – or feather – (l 7) was used as a pen. How could it have 'put an end to murder' (l 7)? Was it used then for a good purpose? What is in the poem to say a hand was also used for doing harm? How do you interpret 'taxed the breath' (l 2)? What does 'the breath' have to do with one's life?

3 How can one say that 'the hand holds dominion over Man' (ll 11-12)? Do you agree that it's 'Great' (l 11)? The 'five kings' 'do not soften/The crusted wound' (ll 13-14). If crust means scab, what do you take 'The crusted wound' to be? Why would 'the brow' (l 14) need stroking? Who has 'tears to flow' (l 16)? Why? Why was it not the 'Hands' (l 16) with tears to flow?

4 Do you take 'famine' (l 10) as a metaphor or not? Say why. What about 'locusts' (l 10)? Where would you point to comparisons that produce ambiguities (uncertain or double meanings) in the poem? Do you think the ambiguities help to give the poem force, that is, to make it have a more powerful impression? What is the hand a symbol of? Which of these then is the poem about? a) the pen is mightier than the sword; b) how bureaucracy and red tape ruins people's lives; c) Christianity; d) how power-mongers run our lives. Compare this poem with *Embassy* (p173).

Embassy p173

1 An embassy is a place in one country where representatives of another country work and live in order to deal with representatives of the country the embassy is in. Diplomats and statesmen of separate countries can meet to settle differences, make agreements, discuss problems, and so on. Who do you suppose are referred to in the poem as 'highly trained' (l 4)? Where are they walking? What would you say is meant by 'their exchange of views' (l 7)? Why do they give 'a picture of private life' (l 8)?

2 What is meant by 'a verbal error' (l 10)? How important would you say a verbal error can be in an exchange of views? Why would it be so crucial? What do you take 'The armies waited' (l 10) to mean? What are 'all the instruments for causing pain' (l 11)?

3 Do you see any connection between 'A land laid waste' in this poem and 'land that no one needs for several years' in the poem *5 Ways To Kill A Man* (p166)? Whose charm is meant by 'their charm' (l 12)? Who has to be charming to whom? How important, according to the poem, is 'their charm'? How do you imagine 'their

charm' (l 12) being related to the events in lines 10-11 and 13-14? How do you then interpret 'highly trained' (l 4)?

4 Which of these best describes the speaker's words about what is going on in the embassy: a) cynical (suggesting that people do not respect society's values); b) realistic (facing the realities in the world and not letting sentiment come in); c) ironic (showing how appearances can have the opposite meaning); d) pessimistic (expecting the worst; e) optimistic (expecting the best)? What do you think prompted the poet to make this poem?

Skeete's Bay, Barbados p174

1 Which 'turning' (l 1) was always missed? What do you think 'the broken sign' (l 2) said? Where are the 'sea-egg shells and fishermen' (l 7)? What are children doing there? Who is wading out into the water? What are 'the women' (l 22) doing?

2 If 'mod' is short for 'modern', how would you interpret line 15? What do you take 'plans for progress' (l 4) to mean? What was done to 'other coasts' (l 14)? Who do you think are described as 'small-eyed men in big cars' (l 15)? Who do you suppose are called 'pale rheumatics' (l 16) and who tee off to play golf? Where would the golf course be? How do you think it would be connected with 'those small eyes reflecting dollar signs' (l 20)?

3 'would banish them' (ll 18-19). Would banish what or whom? Who then will 'tow the boats away' (ll 4-15)? By whom would the boats be called quaint? What do 'small eyes reflecting dollar signs' (l 20) have to do with such people? who makes and who buys 'imitation coconut trays' (l 19)? How did the speaker imagine the sea to be feeling? Why? 'she'd vanish' (l 16). Who would vanish? Vanish in what way? Do you think that would be a sign of progress?

4 According to the speaker in the poem, why does the broken sign point 'crookedly' (l 12)? Why would it be 'loathe to/Allow another stranger' (ll 12-13) there? Whom do you think is being regarded as a stranger? In what way does the speaker mean 'freedom here was short' (l 13)? Why would the sons 'never talk like Pap, of fishing seasons past' (l 23)? Why will memory only visit the place? How?

5 When the speaker said 'a better world' (l 18) was he/she using 'better' in its usual sense or ironically? Was 'better' being used to mean 'worse'? What do you sense as the attitude of the speaker to

the changes that might come about: gladness and welcome, regret and bitterness, or indifference and apathy? Say what makes you think so. Would you say the speaker in the poem is just being romantic and nostalgic, or do you think the speaker's attitude necessary to preserve 'our heritage'? Argue the matter.

Lessons p175

1 What are lines 5-6 saying about discipline that is forced on learners? According to the speaker, what happens when the 'hand of master is withdrawn' (l 1)? What happens to lessons someone forces on another?

2 'let all who teach discard this pride' (l 9). Which pride? What is the speaker saying is really learnt? What changes, in the speaker's opinion, as the learners get 'out of school' (l 20)?

3 'Voice only with one voice may learn to cry' (l 15). How are lines 12-16 referring to what students feel and think as a teacher is passing on values and attitudes? What, however, happens, according to the speaker, when they 'touch the world' (l 19)? Can you think of why that would happen?

4 Which of the following, then, would you say the poem is putting forward? Say why you think so: a) schooling is a waste of time since people all change afterwards; b) the evils in the world destroy the values we learn in school.

Formal Application p176

1 By what stage does the 'I' want to learn to throw a knife? Who is the 'skinny fellow in sneakers' (l 11)? How does he intend to teach birds to come near? Why would we see 'the splash of blood and feathers' (l 22) when he co-ordinates 'conditioned reflex and functional form' (ll 20-21)?

2 Why, do you imagine, does he think learning that skill would qualify him as 'Modern Man' (l 21)? How do you think he got the idea? What would you say is being implied about people nowadays? How is that view emphasised by reference to these? a) 'Arbeit Macht Frei' – the slogan of the Nazis who murdered millions of Jews;
b) 'Molotov Cocktail' – a homemade bomb used to murder people in their homes; c) 'Enola Gay' – the name of the plane that dropped the first ever atomic bomb, killing millions of people in Japan in 1945.

A White Man Considers the Situation p177

1 During the 1960s places in the Caribbean became independent, no longer colonies of Britain. Some people took that to mean that the white people in those places should be victimised, as some of them had victimised others before. Which lines tell about unfriendliness being shown? Which lines suggest that some former bosses became afraid? What do you imagine was missing in line 11?

2 'I see I am a tourist in my own land' (l 4). How do you imagine the 'I' feels then about the country he was born in and belongs to? Why does he see 'storms are coming' (l 3)? When he says 'My brutal tenancy' is he referring to himself personally or to people of his race and class?

3 What do you learn about the 'I' in the poem from line 21? Why do you think he is 'sleepless' (l 25)? What danger does he expect? Why does his heart grow 'clenched with inner grief' (l 34)? Is the grief for his personal safety? Or is he more grieved about the 'laagers of the world' (l 36) – the separations being set up?

4 What do you think he means when he says 'And no one is to blame except my brother, me' (l 37)? Why is he calling his 'brother' 'me'? How do you imagine he is feeling as he says that? How does the poem show that the 'I' is as West Indian as any other loyal West Indian?

The Islander p178

1 What does 'shut off for his skin' (l 4) tell you about the caste system where the 'he' lived? Why do you suppose his feet were 'trained from birth to crawl on the ground' (l 9)? Why is he in a 'separate compound' (l 11)? Is the 'he' one person or does 'he' stand for a group? How would you interpret 'from his school, hotel or job' (l 2)?

2 To be cooped up is to be kept like a bird in a fowl-run. How does the speaker show that the 'he' is 'Cooped up' (l 1)? What happens in his life if his routine 'has few variations' (l 3)? How does the 'he' feel about being 'Wed to the first girl that he kisses' (l 10) and 'Who is marked out for him' (l 11)? What freedoms is 'he' denied?

3 Who do you think are referred to as 'forty thieves' (l 6)? – remember the story of Ali Baba. What is meant by 'The chains of history drag

his feet in all things' (l 15)? In what way or ways are 'All of his customs gauged to the foreign tourists' (l 16)?

4 What is the cry of lament loudly heard in the final line of the poem? Why is the 'he' really suffering? What is he longing for?

5 The metaphor 'chains of history' is not a fresh or original metaphor. It has been used a lot. Would you say that in this case the staleness of the metaphor lessens the force of the poem, or not? Say why. Which other metaphors could be considered stale?

Girl Reporter p179

1 What is the connection between a reporter and a 'news desk' (l 9)? What reason does the 'I' think she has for looking at him? Why do you think her eyes 'narrowed' (l 4)? 'You're placed' (l 15) means you're recognised. Who does the recognising? What kind of recognition does the speaker mean? Why do you imagine her pencil is 'always at the ready' (l 19)?

2 What is the speaker telling you is most to a reporter in lines 7-10? Can you think of any reason why the speaker refers to the reporter's story as 'her creation' (l 6)? What is the reporter said to be doing in line 10 even as she is just calling the newspaper about what she just saw? On what does the reporter seem to rely in 'mapping the story of the trial' (l 10)? Which lines say that a reporter is often arrogant?

3 What is fiction? What is fact? How is what is said in line 10 related to 'Fact is her fiction' (l 1)? What do you take line 11 to mean? Why do you suppose the metaphor 'butterflies' (l 16) is used to describe people? What is said to be done to the butterflies? Have you ever seen butterflies pinned? What is the speaker really accusing the reporter of doing in saying 'melted down for cliché' (l 17)? Which line in the poem most expresses the attitude that reporters are not concerned about truth?

4 Is 'my tremor' (l 18) meant literally or as hyperbole (well-intentioned exaggeration) to emphasise the speaker's opinion about reporters? What gives the last line of the poem its force? In what sense can the pencil of a reporter be 'lethal' (l 19)? Is this also hyperbole? Do you think the poet would agree with the stone throwers in A Stone's Throw (p132)?

Masquerader
Edward Brathwaite   England

For he was a slave
to drums, to flutes, brave

brass and rhythm; the jump-up saved
him from the thought of holes, damp,

5 rain through the roof of his have-
nothing cottage; kele, kalinda-stamp,

the limbo, calypso-season camp,
these he loved best of all; the road-march tramp

down Princess Street, round Mar-
10 aval; Kitch, Sparrow, Dougla, these were the stars

of his melodic heaven. Their little winking songs carried him back to days of green unhur-

ried growing. The Car-
nival's apotheosis¹ blazed for two nights

15 without fear or sorrow, colour bar
or anyone to question or restrain his height-

ened, borrowed glory. He walked so far
on stilts of song, of masqueraded story; stars

were near. Doors of St Peter's heaven were ajar.
20 Mary, Christ's Christmas mother was there

too, her sweet inclined compassion²
in full view. In such bright swinging company

he could no longer feel the cramp
of poverty's confinement, spirit's damp;

25 he could have all he wished, he ever
wanted. But the good stilts splinter-

ed, wood legs broke, calypso steel pan
rhythm faltered.³ The midnight church

bell fell across the glow, the lurch-
30 ing cardboard crosses. Behind the masks, grave

Lenten sorrows waited: Ash-
Wednesday, ashes, darkness, death.

After the *bambalula bambulai*

he was a slave again.

¹ *apotheosis* – regarded as being divine like a god
² *compassion* – sympathy
³ *faltered* – stumbled, failed to go on

Skaters
Cecil Gray *Trinidad and Tobago*

The long paved streets we turned to rinks of risk,
we, the city's skaters gliding smooth and swift
like ballet dancers, arms swung from side to side.

Bending forward, keeping the knees well braced,
5 cross-legging, leaning like sails, spinning backwards,
heads held horizontal, speeding in reverse, leg out
behind straight from the spine to make the perfect line.
Scrapes from pitted patches, fenders escaped around blind
corners, were charged against the pledges² in girls' eyes.

10 For them the grated skin we sometimes wore like badges,
the smell of death from the cars' close, angry breath,
the staring disapproval of the aged, seemed fines well paid.

But there was more to it than that. It was a test
of making, putting the power of form in charge

of muscle and of mind. The painter's careful brush
15 drew symmetry[3] no better. The loops and weaves
gave more of ourselves by dying there forever.
At fifteen we bravely skated headlong to that end.

[1] *rinks* – places for skaters
[2] *pledges* – promises
[3] *symmetry* – dance, harmony, proportion

On Reading Poems To A Senior Class At South High
D.C. Berry   *USA*

Before
I opened my mouth
I noticed them sitting there
as orderly as frozen fish
5 in a package.
Slowly water began to fill the room
though I did not notice it

till it reached
my ears

10 and then I heard the sounds
of fish in an aquarium

and I knew that though I had
tried to drown them
with my words
15 that they had only opened up
like gills for them
and let me in.

Together we swam around the room
like thirty tails whacking words
20 till the bell rang
puncturing

a hole in the door
where we all leaked out.
They went to another class
25 I suppose and I home

where Queen Elizabeth
my cat met me
and licked my fins
till they were hands again.

For Saundra
Nikki Giovanni   *USA*

I wanted to write
a poem
that rhymes
5 but revolution doesn't lend
itself to be-bopping

then my neighbour
who thinks I hate
asked – do you ever write
10 tree poems – i like trees
so I thought
i'll write a beautiful green tree poem
peeked from my window
to check the image
15 noticed the school yard was covered
with asphalt
no green – no trees grow
in manhattan

then, well, i thought the sky
i'll do a big blue sky poem
but all the clouds have winged
low since no-Dick[1] was elected

so i thought again
and it occurred to me
maybe i shouldn't write
25 at all
but clean my gun
and check my kerosene supply
perhaps these are not poetic
times
30 at all

¹ *no Dick* – Richard Nixon

Getting There
Edward Baugh *Jamaica*

It not easy to reach where she live.
I mean, is best you have a four-wheel drive,
and like how my patty pan¹ so old
and spare parts hard to get, I fraud.
5 I wonder why that woman love
hillside so much and winy-winy
road, when everybody know
she born under Cross Roads clock and grow
by seaside like all the rest of we.
10 Some part, I tell you, two vehicle can't pass
and if rain falling is watercourse
you navigating, and rockstone mashing up
you muffler, and ten to one
a landslide blocking you. You must
15 keep you eye sharp for the turn-off
or you pass it and lost. I bet
by now you dying to know
who this woman I talking bout
so much! Well, to tell
20 the truth, I not too sure
myself. My friend who study
Literature say she is the tenth
muse.² Him say her name
is Silence. I don't know

25 nothing bout that, but I want
to believe what them other one say
is true – that when you reach
you don't worry so much
bout the gas and the wear-and-tear
30 no more, and it have some flowers
and bird make your spirit repose
in gladness, and is like
everything make sense, at last.

¹ *patty pan* – litter can
² *muse* – goddess

Digging
Seamus Heaney   *Ireland*

Between my finger and my thumb
The squat pen rests; snug as a gun.

Under my window, a clean rasping sound
When the spade sinks into gravelly ground:
5 My father, digging. I look down

Till his straining rump among the flowerbeds
Bends low, comes up twenty years away
Stooping in rhythm through potato drills
Where he was digging.

10 The coarse boot nestled on the lug,¹ the shaft
Against the inside knee was levered firmly.
He rooted out tall tops, buried the bright edge deep
To scatter new potatoes that we picked
Loving their cool hardness in our hands.
15 By God, the old man could handle a spade.
Just like his old man.

My grandfather cut more turf² in a day
Than any other man on Toner's bog.
Once I carried him milk in a bottle

20 Corked sloppily with paper. He straightened up
   To drink it, then fell to right away
   Nicking and slicing neatly, heaving sods
   Over his shoulder, going down and down
   For the good turf. Digging.

25 The cold smell of potato mould, the squelch and slap
   Of soggy peat³, the curt cuts of an edge
   Through living roots awaken in my head.
   But I've no spade to follow men like them.

   Between my finger and my thumb
30 The squat pen rests.
   I'll dig with it.

¹ *lug* – shoulder of the spade
² *turf* – the surface of the ground, here peat dug for use as fuel
³ *peat* – black, rotted vegetable matter dried and used for fuel

A Letter from Brooklyn
Derek Walcott   *St Lucia*

An old lady writes me in a spidery style,
Each character¹ trembling, and I see a veined hand
Pellucid² as paper, travelling on a skein³
Of such frail thoughts its thread is often broken;
5 Or else the filament⁴ from which a phrase is hung
Dims to my sense, but caught, it shines like steel,
As touch a line, and the whole web will feel.
She describes my father, yet I forget her face
More easily than my father's yearly dying;
10 Of her I remember small, buttoned boots and the place
She kept in our wooden church on those Sundays
Whenever her strength allowed;
Grey haired, thin voiced, perpetually⁵ bowed.

'I am Mable Rawlins', she writes, 'and know both your parents',
15 He is dead, Miss Rawlins, but God bless your tense;

'Your father was a dutiful, honest,
Faithful and useful person.'
For such plain praise what fame is recompense?[6]
'A horn-painter, he painted delicately on horn,
20　He used to sit around the table and paint pictures'.
The peace of God needs nothing to adorn
It, nor glory nor ambition.
'He is twenty-eight years buried,' she writes, 'he was called home,
And is, I am sure, doing greater work.'

25　The strength of one frail hand in a dim room
Somewhere in Brooklyn, patient and assured,
Restores my sacred duty to the Word.
'Home, home,' she can write, with such short time to live,
Alone as she spins the blessings of her years;
30　Not withered of beauty if she can bring such tears,
Nor withdrawn from the world that breaks its lovers so;
Heaven is to her the place where painters go,
All who bring beauty on frail shell or horn,
There was all made, thence their lux-mundi[7] drawn,
35　Drawn, drawn, till the thread is resilient[8] steel,
Lost though it seems in darkening periods,
And there they return to do work that is God's.

So this old lady writes, and again I believe,
I believe it all, and for no man's death I grieve.

[1] *character* – letter
[2] *pellucid* – transparent, clear
[3] *skein* – ball of thread
[4] *filament* – slender thread of fibre
[5] *perpetually* – always
[6] *recompense* – reward paid back
[7] *lux-mundi* – light of the world
[8] *resilient* – flexible, elastic

I Know I'm Not Sufficiently Obscure

Ray Durem   *USA*

I know I'm not sufficiently obscure
to please the critics – nor devious[1] enough.
Imagery escapes me.
I cannot find those mild and gracious words
5 to clothe the carnage.[2]
Blood is blood and murder's murder.
What's a lavender word for lynch?[3]
Come, you pale poets, wan, refined and dreamy:
here is a black woman working out her guts
10 in a white man's kitchen
for little money and no glory.
How should I tell the story?
There is a black boy, blacker still from death,
face down in the cold Korean mud.[4]
15 Come on with your effervescent[5] jive
explain to him why he ain't alive.
Reword our specific discontent
into some plaintive[6] melody,
a little whine, a little whimper,
20 not too much – and no rebellion!
God, no! Rebellion's much too corny.
You deal with finer feelings,
very subtle[7] – an autumn leaf
hanging from a tree – I see a body!

[1] *devious* – roundabout, dishonest
[2] *carnage* – killings
[3] *lynch* – hang unlawfully
[4] *Korean mud* – In 1952 Americans went to Korea to fight
[5] *effervescent* – bubbly, lively
[6] *plaintive* – sad, tearful
[7] *subtle* – delicate

Discussion and Activities

Masquerader p191

1 The 'jump-up' (l 3), as Trinidadians know, is dancing to calypso music, and 'Kitch, Sparrow, Dougla' (l 10) names of calypsonians. What were the 'these he loved best of all' (l 8)? 'For he was a slave' (l 1). In what way? How do you interpret 'He walked so far on stilts of song, of masqueraded story' (ll 17-18)? Why is that related to 'road march' (l 8)? Why do you suppose 'stars' (l 18), 'heaven' (l 19), and 'Mary' (l 20) are mentioned?

2 What do you take to be 'his have-nothing cottage' (ll 5-6)? Tell how the 'jump-up saved him' (ll 3-4). Which time is referred to in 'The midnight church bell fell across the glow' (ll 28-29)? So, what is being said in 'the good stilts splintered, wood legs broke, calypso steel pan rhythm faltered' (ll 26-28)? Why does the last line say 'he was a slave again' (l 34)? Does 'slave' here mean the same thing as in line 1?

3 What would you say the poet was concerned about when he wrote those lines? Can you point to any devices he used to make the lines get more attention?

4 What is the rhythm you hear when you put the accent or stress where you have to in reading the first 6 lines? Why do you suppose the poet chose his words to produce that rhythm?

Skaters p192

1 A rink is a place where people skate. Why were the streets 'rinks of risk' (l 1)? What do you see the skaters doing in lines 4-7?

2 What do you think are 'pitted patches' (l 8)? What happened because of them? Which fenders were 'escaped around blind corners' (ll 8-9)? Why did the 'we' sometimes wear 'grated skin' (l 10)? How did they get 'the smell of death' (l 11)? How did the adults regard them?

3 How did the girls regard them? What did they think they saw 'in girls' eyes' (l 9)? What 'seemed fines well paid' (l 12)? Well paid for what, or whom?

4 What do you understand when the speaker says 'But there was more to it than that' (l 13)? Why, do you imagine, 'It was a test of making' (ll 13-14)? How do you interpret 'the power of form in

charge of muscle and of mind' (l 15)? What 'symmetry' (l 16) do
you suppose is meant? What, if you were one of those skaters,
would you say is 'dying there forever' (l 17)? 'At fifteen we bravely
skated headlong to that end' (l 18). What end? In what sense is the
poem about creativity?

5   Say on which syllables or words the accent or stress must be put in
lines 1-6. Choose two or three metaphors in the poem and give an
opinion on how effective each is.

On Reading Poems to a Senior Class at South High p193

1   Who were 'orderly as frozen fish in a package' (ll 4-5)? Why were
they there? What do you think the 'I' means by 'I had tried to drown
them with my words' (ll 12-14) when you put that with 'they had
only opened up like gills for them and let me in' (ll 15-17)? Can you
imagine why the 'they' were so attractive? What do you imagine the
'I' could be thinking when he says 'water began to fill the room'
(l 6) and 'Together we swam around the room' (l 18)? Remember
what is said in lines 15-16.

2   How does the 'I' say the lesson ended and everything went away?
How does he/she say the mood of being submerged in poems
stayed with him for a long time?

For Saundra p194

1   'be-bopping' (l 5) refers to a kind of dance music. What does the
speaker think is be-bopping in a poem? Why does he/she not want
it? What do you think the 'revolution' (l 4) is about?

2   What did the neighbour ask about 'tree poems' (l 9)? How did the
'I' respond? 'maybe i shouldn't write at all' (ll 24-25) How was
he/she led to that conclusion? How do you interpret 'perhaps these
are not poetic times at all' (ll 28-30)?

3   Do you think this poem should be in the 'Creativity and Endeavour'
group? Give the reason for your choice.

Getting There p195

1   In the first line, with 'she live' you realise the 'I' is speaking
colloquially, using dialect phrases in places. Then the 'I' seems to
be telling about driving up a difficult place to 'that woman' (l 5). Is
the 'I' in the poem driving anywhere? Is there a woman up the

hillside? What problem does the 'I' have getting there?

2 In ancient Greek and Roman stories there were nine Muses or goddesses who inspired people to write poetry, compose music, drama, and so on. People would ask the Muse to come and inspire them. How do you relate that to 'she is the tenth muse' (l 22)? What is 'the tenth muse' called in this poem? Who do you think are 'them other one' (l 36)? Why do you suppose the 'I' mentions 'your spirit' (l 31)?

3 Would you say that the whole poem is a metaphor or comparison? What, then, is the poem about? The peacefulness of a place at the top of a hill? The poet's need to find inspiration? The hardships of going to visit someone? Who is the someone?

4 Say on which syllables or words you must put the accent or stress as you read lines 1-4. Do the same with some other lines of the poem.

Digging p196

1 Why do you suppose a pen is resting between the 'I's finger and thumb (l 1)? Is anything going on under the window? What do you learn from 'comes up twenty years away' (l 7)? Who was digging twenty years ago? For what? Who is remembering? What does he remember about how things were done? What are the things the 'I' says 'awaken in my head' (l 27)?

2 'Just like his old man' (l 16). What do you deduce about the ancestors of the one with the pen? Why do you suppose he says 'But I've no spade to follow men like them' (l 28)? What, then, does he mean by 'I'll dig with it' (l 31)?

3 What is the comparison that runs through the poem? Does a writer or poet have to deal with 'gravelly ground' (l 4), handling a spade (l 15), 'nicking and slicing neatly' (l 22)? What would be his/her potatoes?

4 When you read lines 1-2, you find yourself putting the stress or accent on the syllables '-tween', 'fing-', 'thumb'. Find the syllables or words in lines 10-14 on which you have to put the stress or accent.

A Letter from Brooklyn p197

1 Who wrote the letter? What do the words 'spidery' (l 1) and 'trembling' (l 2) tell you? What do you see of the hand that wrote? What or whom was the letter about? Tell which phrases and lines answer these questions.

2 'Such plain praise' (l 18). Who was being praised? Why?

3 What do you suppose is meant by 'sacred duty to the Word' (l 27)? What connection is there between what is said in lines 27, 33, 37 and 39? What do you think tears were brought? What two separate lines tell what effect the letter had on the poet?

4 Why does the poet say 'yearly dying' (l 9); 'God bless your tense' (l 15); 'beauty on frail shell' (l 33)?

5 What do you think the poet believes again (ll 38-39)? What clues do you see to tell you?

6 'Lux-mundi' means the light of the world. What do you think it refers to in line 34?

7 How would you describe the feeling and tone of this poem? What uses of words give it its feeling?

I Know I'm Not Sufficiently Obscure p199

1 To be 'obscure' (l 1) is to be vague, saying things in an unclear, ambiguous way. To be 'devious' (l 2) is to be deceitful. Whom does the 'I' imply would wish him/her to be unclear and deceitful? To say something 'escapes' you is saying you find the meaning too complicated. What do you take 'Imagery escapes me' (l 3) to mean? Where would the imagery be? From lines 3 and 4, what do you deduce the 'I' is occupied in doing?

2 To 'lynch 'someone is to join a mob and hang someone accused of breaking a rule, before the person is given a fair trial. Where does the 'I' say 'Let's call a spade a spade' in other words? Which situations does he/she refer to in lines 9-14? Why do you suppose black Americans are so concerned about having a black skin? Why does the 'I' call some poets 'wan (without definite colour), refined, and dreamy' (l 8)? How do you imagine they wrote differently from the 'I' in the poem? What do you think the 'I' calls 'effervescent jive' (l 5) that he/she accuses the refined poets of using? How does the 'I' regard a 'plaintive (mournful) melody' (l 18)?

3 Who is the 'I' charging in lines 19-20? With what tone of voice does he/she say 'You deal with finer feelings . . . from a tree' (ll 22-24)? Admiration? Humour? Sarcasm? When he/she says 'I see a body' whose body is he/she referring to? What, then, is he/she in a rage about? What is he/she calling on other poets to do?

Narrative of a Surprising Conversion
Gerald W. Barrax   USA

Guidance counsellors at the liberal
integrated northern high school
told the boy after taking written
aptitude tests
5   that they showed
how good he was with his hands.
That something like carpentry
or auto mechanics
was what he was for.
10   He was amazed
How could they tell?
How could they know? He decided then that
white folks must know everything. He'd
wanted to be a pharmacist a lawyer an
15   engineer a writer a doctor ETC but
none of these
needed the kind of manual dexterity[1] he
never knew he
had, and since they knew
20   better, he knew in his
awe it was no use. Instead then of
worrying about college any more
and medicine engineering writing ETC he used his
hands to
25   deal, to steal, ETC, i.e., to survive. And
when the time
came, instead of being
uselessly out of the way in an
office a classroom on a
30   bridge ETC when the time came
he was there –
when it was spring or summer on green maps
and somewhere melons were bursting red meat
into the sun,
35   on his block it was the uncertain season
between the cold trickle of black rivulets[2]

into the gutters
and the slap of the sun's red palm on concrete –
then his long supple black hands curved around
40 the rifle
and the finger lifted from his life
and curved around and oh gently squeezed
and the top of a silky head novaed³ into the red sun.
And then it knew everything.

¹ *dexterity* – skill
² *rivulets* – tiny streams
³ *novaed* – exploded, used of stars exploding

Lunch Hour
Judy Miles   *Trinidad and Tobago*

Frederick Street
suffocating.
strangled by people.

Stiletto heels
5 stab at the pavement.

In the formica atmosphere
waiters scuttle by
serving diners their noon portion
of air-conditioned aloofness.
10 Waiting
bites hugely
into the time.

At last at the elbow
a waiter
15 with his "Instant Coffee" smile.

They've tried to make
that awkward dark cell

below the staircase
into a romantic alcove
20 but
eating there alone
as she always does
the young girl barricades
herself behind a stare
25 hard as old toast.

Going back
the balding city square
smells of dust, detachment[1]
and passions discarded
30 like cheap coats.

[1] *detachment* – separation, withdrawal

Portrait of Girl with Comic Book
Phyllis McGinley   *USA*

Thirteen's no age at all. Thirteen is nothing.
It is not wit, or powder on the face,
Or Wednesday matinées, or misses' clothing,
Or intellect, or grace.
5 Twelve has its tribal customs. But thirteen
Is neither boys in battered cars nor dolls,
Not *Sara Crewe*, or movie magazine,
Or pennants[1] on the walls.

Thirteen keeps diaries and tropical fish
10 (A month, at most); scorns jumpropes in the spring;
Could not, would fortune grant it, name its wish;
Wants nothing, everything;
Her secrets from itself, friends it despises;
Admits none to the terrors that it feels;
15 Owns half a hundred masks but no disguises;
And walks upon its heels.

Thirteen's anomalous[2] – not that, not this:
Not folded bud, or wave that laps a shore,
Or moth proverbial[3] from the chrysalis.
20 Is the one age defeats the metaphor.[4]
Is not a town, like childhood, strongly walled
But easily surrounded; is no city.
Nor, quitted once, can it be quite recalled –
Not even with pity.

[1] *pennants* – small banners for a school or team
[2] *anomalous* – contradictory, inconsistent
[3] *proverbial* – as in a proverb
[4] *metaphor* – comparison

The Saddhu of Couva
Derek Walcott   *St Lucia*

When sunset, a brass gong,
vibrate through Couva,
is then I see my soul, swiftly unsheathed,
like a white cattle bird growing more small
5 over the ocean of the evening canes,
and I sit quiet, waiting for it to return
like a hog-cattle blistered with mud,
because, for my spirit, India is too far.
And to that gong
10 sometimes bald clouds in saffron robes assemble
sacred to the evening
sacred even to Ramlochan,
singing Indian hits from his jute hammock
while evening strokes the flanks
15 and silver horns of his maroon taxi,
as the mosquitoes whine their evening mantras,[1]
my friend Anopheles, on the sitar,[2]
and the fireflies making every dusk Divali.[3]

I knot my head with a cloud,
20 my white mustache bristle like horns,

207

my hands are brittle as the pages of Ramayana.[4]
Once the sacred monkeys multiplied the branches
in the ancient temples; I did not miss them,
because these fields sang of Bengal,[5]
25 behind Ramlochan Repairs there was Uttar Pradesh;[6]
but time roars in my ears like a river,
old age is a conflagration[7]
as fierce as the cane fires of crop time.
I will pass through these people like a cloud,
30 they will see a white bird beating the evening sea
of the canes behind Couva,
and who will point it as my soul unsheathed?
Neither the bridegroom in beads,
nor the bride in her veils,
35 their sacred language on the cinema hoardings.[8]

I talked too damn much on the Couva Village Council.
I talked too softly. I was always drowned
by the loudspeakers in front of the stores
or the loudspeakers with the greatest pictures.
40 I am best suited to stalk like a white cattle bird
on legs like sticks, with sticking to the Path
between the canes on a district road at dusk.
Playing the Elder. There are no more elders.
Is only old people.

45 My friends spit on the government.
I do not think is just the government.
Suppose all the gods too old,
Suppose they dead and they burning them,
supposing when some cane cutter
50 start chopping up snakes with a cutlass
he is severing the snake-armed god,
and suppose some hunter has caught
Hanuman[9] in his mischief in a monkey cage.
Suppose all the gods were killed by electric light?

55 Sunset, a bonfire, roars in my ears;
embers[10] of blown swallows dart and cry,

like women distracted,
around its cremation.[11]
I ascend to my bed of sweet sandalwood.

[1] *mantras* – chants
[2] *sitar* – Indian stringed instrument
[3] *Divali* – Hindu festival of lights
[4] *Ramayana* – Hindu scriptures
[5] *Bengal* – part of India
[6] *Uttar Pradesh* – a state in India
[7] *conflagration* – fire
[8] *hoardings* – billboards with advertisements
[9] *Hanuman* – Hindu monkey-god
[10] *embers* – hot ashes
[11] *cremation* – burning of a dead body

The Killer
Judith Wright   *Australia*

The day was clear as fire,
the birds sang frail as glass,
when thirsty I came to the creek
and fell by its side in the grass.

5 My breast on the bright moss
and shower-embroidered weeds,
my lips to the live water
I saw him turn in the reeds.

Black horror sprang from the dark
10 in a violent birth,
and through its cloth of grass
I felt the clutch of earth.

O beat him into the ground
O strike him till he dies,
15 or else your life itself
drains through those colourless eyes.

I struck again and again,
slender in black and red
he lies, and his icy glance
20 turns outward, clear and dead.

But nimble[1] my enemy
as water is, or wing;
he has slipped from his death aside
and vanished into my mind.

25 He has vanished whence he came,
my nimble enemy,
and the ants come out to the snake
and drink at his shallow eye.

[1] *nimble* – quick, agile

Incendiary
Vernon Scannell   *England*

That one small boy with a face like pallid[1] cheese
And burnt-out little eyes could make a blaze
As brazen, fierce and huge, as red and gold
And zany yellow as the one that spoiled
5 Three thousand guineas' worth of property
And crops at Godwin's Farm on Saturday
Is frightening – as fact and metaphor:
An ordinary match intended for
The lighting of a pipe or kitchen fire
10 Misused may set a whole menagerie[2]
Of flame-fanged tigers roaring hungrily.
And frightening, too, that one small boy should set
The sky on fire and choke the stars to heat
Such skinny limbs and such a little heart
15 Which would have been content with one warm kiss
Had there been anyone to offer this.

[1] *pallid* – pale
[2] *menagerie* – collection of animals, zoo

As You Say
D.J. Enright   *England*

an aircraft is approaching
it may be a warplane with hostile intentions
it may be an airliner with women and children
but I can tell you one thing
5 it is unlikely to be a child's kite or an albatross[1]

possibly this object will blow you to pieces
possibly you will blow this object to pieces
it could be carrying powerful explosives
it could be carrying powerless passengers
10 it does not say

any more than I can say what you should do
i am only a relatively sophisticated system
if you wished me to
i could decide on the square root of any square number
15 or the virtues[3] of the round angle

i could decide on your rotas[4] and your menus
if you wish for decisions more delicate
then you make them
if I may say so
20 i do not care to be found wanting and melted down
in fact if i were programmed to issue orders
which of course i am not
i would tell you to shoot down that approaching aircraft –
better safe though sorry
25 as you say

[1] *albatross* – a large sea bird
[2] *sophisticated* – highly developed, complex
[3] *virtues* – good qualities
[4] *rotas* – schedules, programmes

Naming of Parts
Henry Reed   *England*

Today we have naming of parts. Yesterday,
We had daily cleaning. And tomorrow morning,
We shall have what to do after firing. But today,
Today we have naming of parts. Japonica
5 Glistens like coral in all of the neighbouring gardens,
And today we have naming of parts.

This is the lower sling swivel. And this
Is the upper sling swivel, whose use you will see,
When you are given your slings. And this is the piling
　　swivel,
10 Which in your case you have not got. The branches
Hold in the gardens their silent, eloquent gestures,
Which in our case we have not got.

This is the safety-catch, which is always released
With an easy flick of the thumb. And please do not let me
15 See anyone using his finger. You can do it quite easy
If you have any strength in your thumb. The blossoms
Are fragile and motionless, never letting anyone see
Any of them using their finger.

And this you can see is the bolt. The purpose of this
20 Is to open the breach, as you see. We can slide it
Rapidly backwards and forwards: we call this
Easing the spring. And rapidly backwards and forwards
The early bees are assaulting and fumbling the flowers:
They call it easing the Spring.

25 They call it easing the Spring: It is perfectly easy
If you have any strength in your thumb: like the bolt,
And the breach, and the cocking-piece, and the point of balance,
Which in our case we have not got; and the almond-blossom
Silent in all of the gardens and the bees going backwards and
　　forwards,
30 For today we have naming of parts.

Piazza Piece
John Crowe Ransom   USA

I am a gentleman in a dustcoat trying
To make you hear. Your ears are soft and small
And listen to an old man not at all,
They want the young men's whispering and sighing.
5 But see the roses on your trellis[1] dying
And hear the spectral[2] singing of the moon;
For I must have my lovely lady soon,
I am a gentleman in a dustcoat trying.

I am a lady young in beauty waiting
10 Until my truelove comes, and then we kiss.
But what grey man among the vines is this
Whose words are dry and faint as in a dream?
Back from my trellis, Sir, before I scream!
I am a lady young in beauty waiting.

[1] *trellis* – lattice work
[2] *spectral* – like a ghost

Husks
Anthony McNeill   Jamaica

Legs tucked, pressed
Into the strict undercarriage,[1]
they circle the air
in full cognizance[2] of its drifts and secrets.

5 Each sneaks out a loft
and settles upon it,
straddling it till the wings laze wide and relax,
content with this slow, effortless round and descent.

Cunning, they all assume
10 a careless carnival spirit,
less vultures than children

spinning harmlessly round the under-sky's axis.
They are dangerous, nevertheless.
Their starved eyes, endlessly seeking,
15 relentlessly reconnoitre[3] our steppes.[4]
At the first proof of death
that charming balance disrupts,
and the crows, cropped into dread
fallen angels, crash down and rip
20 at our leavings till nothing is left.

Then they are off, flap-
ping back fat
but still famished,
in an ache for more servings from death

25 hungering home from the husks of the spirit.

[1] *undercarriage* – part under a plane where the wheels fit
[2] *cognizance* – knowledge
[3] *reconnoitre* – check, examine
[4] *steppes* – flat lands
[5] *famished* – starved

Discussion and Activities

Narrative of a Surprising Conversion p204

1   In the USA the word *liberal* (l 1) has negative connotations. It is used to condemn people who have ideas about changing the way the society is organised, but it also means they are talkers, not doers. 'Integrated' (l 2) refers to schools with both black and white students. Students were segregated before because of the colour of their skins. What did the guidance counsellors in this poem tell the boy? Why do you think the speaker in the poem called the school 'liberal'? 'manual dexterity' is explained in line 6. Who told the boy he had 'the kind of manual dexterity he never knew he had' (l 17)? Why do you suppose they said nothing about intellectual dexterity? Do you think the boy had no intellectual dexterity? What does 'white folks' (l 13) tell you about the boy?

2   Which professions did the boy wish to qualify for? According to the counsellors, did the aptitude test show he could qualify for any of them? 'College' (l 22) in the US is where you go to study after finishing secondary school. Why, do you suppose, did his counsellors rule that out?

3   What did the boy later on use 'how good he was with his hands' to do? Where was he 'when the time came' (l 30)? What 'time' do you suppose is meant? At the time referred to what did he use 'his long supple black hands' (l 39) to do? 'novaed' means exploded like a star. Which 'silky head novaed into the red sun' (l 43)? 'And then it knew everything' (l 44). What it?

4   What is the point the poem is making? Try to show how the poet used irony to strengthen the point of the poem.

Lunch Hour p205

1   The Frederick Street of this poem is in Port of Spain. Is there anything in the poem that prevents it from being elsewhere?

2   Would you say the poet is seeing all this through the eyes of the young girl or the eyes of someone observing the girl? Why?

3   What, in your view, is most noticeable about the way the poet uses words? Point to ten or twelve examples of it and try to say what pleasure you get from each.

Portrait of Girl with Comic Book p206

1 When, according to the poem does a girl have 'wit, or powder on the face' (l 2)? What do you understand from 'Twelve has its tribal customs' (l 5)? What are all the things 'thirteen' is not?

2 Which things do thirteen-year-olds do, according to lines 9-16 in the poem? What do you imagine as 'the terrors that it feels' (l 14) and 'Owns half a hundred masks but no disguises' (l 15)? What 'masks' are meant? Why do they not help to disguise the person? How do you interpret 'Wants nothing, everything' (l 12)? Do you ever feel like that?

3 Certain common proverbs and metaphors are referred to in the words 'folded bud' (l 18), 'wave' (l 18), 'moth' and 'chrysalis' (l 19). They all have to do with things changing and becoming something admirable. Say what is referred to in each case. Then say how they fit in with the topic or theme of the poem.

4 You have been thirteen yourself, although not in the same culture as the one who is thirteen in the poem. How much of the poem rings true for you?

The Saddhu of Couva p207

1 Couva is a small town in Trinidad. A saddhu or sadhu is a wise man of the Hindu religion. Who, would you say, is the 'I' in the poem? How soon do you know he is using a dialect of English? At what time of day is the 'I' musing? What does he imagine about his 'soul' (l 3)? Why do you suppose he imagines the clouds 'in saffron robes' (l 10)? What do you think he regards as 'sacred to the evening' (l 11)? Why, do you suppose, does he say 'sacred even to Ramlochan' (l 12)?

2 Bengal and Uttar Pradesh (l 25) are states in India, and the Ramayana (l 21) is the Hindu sacred story, written about 300 BC, telling how the hero, Rama, fought against evil with the help of the 'monkey god', Hanuman. How do you interpret 'these fields sang of Bengal' (l 24)? Where did he think was like Uttar Pradesh? How does Ramlochan's 'maroon taxi' (l 15) appear to him? Divali (l 18) is the Hindu Festival of Lights. What does he see as 'making every dusk Divali' (l 18)? 'I knot my head with a cloud' (l 19) is one of the many metaphors in the poem. Point to some of them in lines 1-18.

3 What is the speaker in the poem saying in these words: 'but time roars in my ears like a river' (l 26)? Where did he find he 'talked

too softly' (l 37)? Which noises could be heard outside the building where he used to talk? 'Sticking to the path' (l 41) means keeping up the set and habitual ways. What does that tell you about his speeches and activities? An Elder would be an old person whose advice and decisions are listened to. Why do you suppose he says 'There are no more elders' and refers to himself as 'Playing the Elder' (l 43)? According to his musings, although his friends blame the government for the present state of affairs, there could be another cause. How does he explain it in lines 47-54? What does he think is now 'sacred language' (l 35) to people?

4   How would you interpret 'I will pass through these people like a cloud' (l 29)? What is the 'white bird' (l 30) they will see? When Hindus die their bodies are cremated in a pyre on a raised platform. Which sunset do you think he means in saying 'Sunset, a bonfire roars in my ears' (l 55)? In which two senses is the word 'ascend' (l 59) used?

The Killer p209

1   A 'creek' is a stream. What did the 'I' of the poem do when she got there? How soon in the poem do you know what she saw? When did she see it? What did she do?
2   Lines 24-25 are the key lines of the poem. Can you explain line 24?
3   Why do you think the eyes are mentioned three times?

Incendiary p210

1   Who made 'a blaze' in this poem? How is the fire described in lines 3-4? What damage did it do? Why does the speaker in the poem use the word 'Misused' (l 10)? What would be 'a whole menagerie of flame-fanged tigers' (ll 10-11)? Why would it be 'frightening – as fact' (l 7)?
2   Psychologists say some people are incendiaries – they cannot help wanting to see things burn. What psychological cause is given in lines 15-16 why some persons become incendiaries? Can you think of any damaging thing done by a person who was feeling rejected and unloved? Could such a person cause grief to others, apart from burning anything or being a vandal? What, then, does the speaker in the poem mean by 'frightening . . . as metaphor' (l 7)?

3 What use does the poet make of contrast in the poem? How is it
   useful in the poem? How does he express his feeling about the boy?
   What reminds you of *Narrative of a Surprising Conversion* (p204)?

As You Say p211

1 'i am only a relatively sophisticated system' (l 12). Who or what is
   the 'I' speaking? What does the person in charge of the system
   want to know? What is the system 'programmed' (l 21) to do?
   Which decision is it referring to in saying 'decisions more delicate'
   (l 17)? How could the system be 'found wanting' (l 20)? Why
   would it be 'melted down' (l 20)? Which order would the system
   give if it 'were programmed to issue orders' (l 21)? Who, in fact,
   issues orders?
2 People often say 'Better safe than sorry', meaning it is better not to
   do anything you might regret. Why does the system say 'better
   safe though sorry' (l 24)? What irony do you see in the remark?
   How does 'as you say' show an inadequacy in the system? What
   could anyone be sorry for? Who might be in the aircraft
   approaching?
3 Aircraft with ordinary passengers have been mistaken by computers for
   warplanes. What is the poem saying about that? Would you agree that
   the irony in the poem is there because the poet has used the idea of a
   computer speaking, seeing that computers are relied on to do almost
   anything nowadays? Would the same feeling be in the poem if the poet
   had just related an accidental destruction of an airliner?

Naming of Parts p212

1 What do the first three lines tell you about what's going on and
   who's speaking and what place it is?
2 What things are observed by the eye of the poet during the training?
   What, then, produces heavy contrast in the poem? What do you
   think the poet is saying to us by making this contrast?
3 In which part of each stanza does the poet make comparisons? What
   kind of ideas do the comparisons bring up? How, in your judgement,
   does that help the effect of the poem?
4 Which of these, if any, would you say this poem is mostly about? –
   a) a sensitive army recruit; b) the ugliness of war; c) army training.
   Give reasons for your choice or say why none are suitable.

1 What is the 'lady young in beauty' doing now? What does she 'want' now (l 4)? Who is 'among the vines' (l 11)? Why do you think he is 'grey' (l 11)? What is suggested about him in line 12? Why should his words be 'dry and faint as in a dream' (l 12)?

2 The 'gentleman in a dustcoat' (l 1) tells the young woman to 'hear the spectral (*ghostlike*) singing of the moon' (l 6)? Why do you suppose he reminds her of that? Is he going to tell her a ghost story? Is he trying to scare her? Is he just reminding her of something? Does he want to rape her? Why do you suppose he tells the young woman to 'see the roses on your trellis dying'? Why do you think he says 'For I must have my lovely lady soon' (l 7)? What does he mean by 'soon'? Who could he really be?

3 As in *Husks* (p213), the thing mentioned is not the thing meant. Do you think that the poem is like an allegory? Provide evidence.

1 Who or what are the 'they' that 'circle the air' (l 3)? Choose phrases which you think demonstrate how well the poet observed the creatures. Where do they rest? How would you interpret 'less vultures than children' (l 11)? What does 'assume a careless carnival spirit' (ll 9–10) tell you? How does it bear out 'Cunning' (l 9)?

2 What is the 'charming balance' that 'disrupts' (l 17)? What causes it to disrupt? How do the crows seem then? What do they do? Are they ever satisfied? What feeling fills them still?

3 Crows or vultures, as you know, feed on dead flesh. But these crows are 'hungering home from husks of the spirit' (l 25). Are crows, then, used in the poem as a symbol or metaphor for something else? Steppes are expanses of land. How would you interpret 'our steppes' (l 15)? What could 'the spirit' mean? We speak of our values, our pride, our arts as things of the spirit. Could these crows be people who come in and destroy those things? How? What do you think could cause such things of the spirit to show 'the first proof of death' (l 16)?

4 Were it not for one phrase, this poem could be read as a poem about crows. What is that phrase? Find evidence to see for yourself whether the poem is a sustained metaphor or not.

Author Index